# THE
# SCRABBLE®
# BOOK

# THE SCRABBLE® BOOK

## GYLES BRANDRETH

TREASURE PRESS

First published in Great Britain in 1984 by
William Collins & Co. Ltd under the title 'The Scrabble Omnibus'

This edition first published in Great Britain in 1990 by
Treasure Press
Michelin House
81 Fulham Road
London SW3 6RB

ISBN 1 85051 514 X

Printed in Yugoslavia

# CONTENTS

# FOREWORD

Scrabble is the world's most popular word game. In my view, it is also the best. I am prejudiced, of course. Scrabble has been a part of my life for as long as I can remember and, I promise you, not a day of my life goes by without my thinking about, talking about or playing Scrabble.

I first played the game in the 1950s when I was quite a small boy. I began to take it seriously when I first went to boarding school in the early 1960s. The school – Bedales, in Hampshire – was a coeducational establishment at which it was the parents – ranging from Oscar Wilde to Princess Margaret via Ramsay Macdonald and Laurence Olivier – who tended to be distinguished rather than the pupils. The school was founded in the 1890s by a great educational pioneer called John Badley and I played Scrabble with him regularly, aged 100. Yes, that was his age, not mine.

By the time I went to Bedales, Mr Badley was no longer the headmaster, but he still lived in a cottage in the grounds and on Wednesday afternoons I would go down and play him at Scrabble. We played scores of games during the year or two I knew him and invariably he won. He won, a) because he was the better player; b) because I had to let him use obsolete words since he insisted they'd been current in his youth; and c) because his housekeeper kept the score and I rather think she cooked the books (she also cooked the scones and had trained as a physiotherapist so I felt it best not to complain). However, I was determined to beat Mr Badley at least once in my life – and his. I went into serious training, made a determined effort to increase my vocabulary and, just as the great man was entering his hundred and second year, I managed to beat him by four points. A month later he was dead. I have hardly dared win a game of Scrabble since.

When I founded the National Scrabble Championships in 1971 I had the pleasure and privilege of meeting another Grand Old Man, Richard Spear, who was then the Chairman of J. W. Spear and Sons and the much-loved elder statesman of the British toys and games industry. Mr Spear was the man who brought Scrabble to Europe and my debt to him and to his son, Francis Spear, who is the present Chairman of the company and who, incidentally, was also a pupil at Bedales (clearly the best schools are Scrabble schools), is enormous. Without them, and their hardworking colleagues at J. W. Spear and Sons, there would be no Scrabble Championships – and no book.

*The Scrabble Omnibus* is the result of my 13 lucky years of involvement with the National Scrabble Championship. As well as providing the rules and history of the game, the book aims to give an insight into how a seasoned Scrabble player's mind works and offers a great variety of games and puzzles, quizzes and challenges specifically designed to improve *your* Scrabble skills. It should even help you play Scrabble in Greek!

I know so much about Scrabble not because I am a wonderful player but because I have so many friends who are. Foremost among these Scrabble gurus is Darryl Francis, a brilliant Scrabble player and an inveterate verbivore, who has been of invaluable help to me in compiling the book. My thanks to him, and to the other Scrabble masters whose ingenuity you will discover in the pages that follow. My thanks, too, to you for reading the book. It is a joy to me that for once in my life I can be 100 per cent certain that my readers are intelligent, civilized and charming. They must be: all Scrabble players are.

**GYLES BRANDRETH**

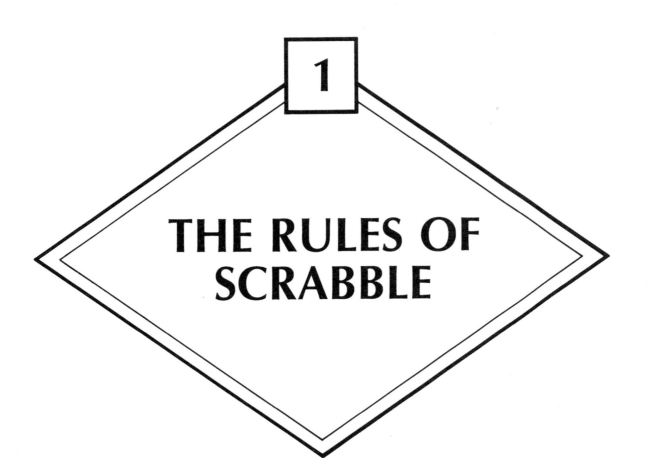

# THE RULES OF SCRABBLE

Scrabble is a word game for two, three or four players. The play consists of forming interlocking words, in a crossword fashion, on the Scrabble board, using letter tiles with various score values. Each player competes for the highest score by using his letters in combinations and locations that take best advantage of letter values and premium squares on the board. The combined total score for a game may range from about 500 to 1,000 points or more, depending on the number of players and their skill.

## TO BEGIN

All the letter tiles should be turned face down at the side of the board or thoroughly mixed in the bag provided. Players draw for first play. The player drawing the letter nearest the beginning of the alphabet plays first. The exposed tiles should then be replaced and reshuffled. Each player then draws seven new tiles and places them on his rack.

## THE PLAY

1.  The first player combines two or more of his letters to form a word and places them on the board to read either across or down. One letter has to be on the pink square marked with an asterisk at the centre of the board. Words cannot be played diagonally.

2.  A player completes his turn by counting and announcing his score for the turn. His score (and the subsequent scores of the other players) should be recorded by one of the players. He then draws as many new letters as he has played, thus keeping seven letters on his rack.

3.  Play passes to the left. The second player, and then each in turn, adds one or more letters to those already played so as to form new words. All letters played in any one turn must be placed in one row across or down the board. They must form one complete word and if, at the same time, they touch other letters in adjacent rows, they must form complete words, crossword fashion, with all such letters. The player gets full credit for all words formed or modified by his play.

4.  New words may be formed by: (a) adding one or more letters to a word or letters already on the board, (b) placing a word at right angles to a word already on the board – the new word must

use one of the letters already on the board or must add a letter to it, or (c) placing a complete word parallel to a word already played so that adjoining letters also form complete words.

5.  The two blank tiles may be used as any letter desired. When playing a blank, the player must state what letter it represents, after which it cannot be changed during the game.

6.  No letter nor a blank may be moved from the board once it has been played.

7.  Any player may use his turn to replace any or all of the letters on his rack. He does so by discarding them face down, then drawing the same number of new letters, and finally mixing the discarded letters with those remaining in the pool. He then awaits his next turn to play.

8.  Play continues until all the tiles have been drawn and one of the players has used all the letters on his rack or until all possible plays have been made.

9.  Any words found in a standard dictionary are permitted except those starting with a capital letter, those designated as foreign words, abbreviations, and words requiring apostrophes or hyphens. A dictionary may be consulted only to check spelling or usage. Any word may be challenged before the next player starts his turn. If the word challenged is unacceptable, the player takes back his tiles and loses his turn.


## SCORING

1.  One player should be selected before the game starts to keep a tally of each player's score.

2.  The score value of each letter is indicated by a number at the bottom of the tile. The score value of the blanks is zero.

3.  *Premium Letter Squares:* A light blue square doubles the score of the letter played on it. A dark blue square triples the score of the letter played on it.

4.  *Premium Word Squares:* The score for the entire word is doubled when one of its letters is placed on a pink square. It is tripled when a letter is placed on a red square. Include premiums for double or triple letter values, if any, before

doubling or tripling the word score. If a word is formed that covers two premium word squares, the score should be doubled and re-doubled (that is, four times the letter count), or tripled and re-tripled (nine times the letter count). Note that the centre square of the board is pink, and therefore doubles the score for the first word played.

5.  The score for each turn is the sum of the score values in each word formed or modified in the play, plus the premium values resulting from placing letters on premium squares.

6.  Letter and word premiums apply only in the turn in which they are first used. In subsequent turns, letters count at face value only.

7.  When a blank tile falls on a pink or red square, the sum of the letters in the word is doubled or tripled even though the blank itself has no score value.

8.  When two or more words are formed in the same turn, each is scored. The common letters are counted, with full premium values if any, in the score for each word.

9.  Any player who plays all seven of his tiles in a single turn scores a premium (or bonus) of 50 points in addition to his regular score for the play.

10.  At the end of the game, each player's score is reduced by the sum of his unplayed letters, and, if one player has used all of his letters, his score is increased by the sum of the unplayed letters of all the other players.

*These rules for playing Scrabble and scoring are taken from the leaflet provided with the game of Scrabble as produced in Great Britain. The rules are published by and copyrighted by J. W. Spear and Sons plc.*

# 2

# THE HISTORY OF SCRABBLE

The game of Scrabble was first commercially produced in the United States in 1949. Prior to its appearance on the market, however, it had had a very long gestation – 18 years or so.

The development of Scrabble goes back to the early 1930s. The game itself was not the brainchild of just one individual, but two. Alfred Butts and James Brunot were the game's progenitors. They were the two people who did most to develop Scrabble, but they had considerable help from family, friends and colleagues.

Alfred Butts had had a lifelong interest in words and word puzzles. He liked to do crosswords and solve anagrams and play with a number of other word puzzles which circulated among a minority in the USA. The Great Depression saw Butts unemployed by 1931, and this left him with a considerable amount of free time. By 1933, Butts had some vague ideas for a game which he called Lexiko. He had investigated the wide variety of commercially-produced games and had discovered that although there were a good number of card games, bingo-type games, and games with pieces and counters, there were no commercial word games. Butts wanted to develop Lexiko into a commercial product, hoping to make some money from it.

In its prototype version, Lexiko had letter tiles and racks, but nothing else. There was no board, and there were no point values on the tiles. The idea of the game was simply to try to make a seven-letter word from the tiles on the rack. If a player could not see a word, he could exchange some of his tiles for others from the pool of unused tiles. This exchange of letters continued until one player was able to build a seven-letter word with his tiles, winning the game.

A later version of Lexiko saw the introduction of point values on the tiles. When a player went out with a seven-letter word, the other players were allowed to make shorter words if they could. The point values on the tiles were then used to score these shorter words, and a ranking was thus obtained for the other players. Butts offered the game to various manufacturers, but none of them was interested.

The crucial step in the development of the game was the board. Butts devised a board with various premium squares, and decided that the players should take it in turns to build words on the board, interlocking in crossword fashion. The players scored points related to the values of the tiles played and the premium squares covered. This was getting pretty close to modern-day Scrabble! Butts went back to the commercial games manufacturers with his modified game, by now called It. Again, it was roundly rejected.

Undaunted, Butts continued tinkering with the game between 1933 and 1938, but he had still not managed to capture the interest of a single manufacturer when, in 1939, he was introduced to Jim Brunot. This vital meeting was brought about by a social worker, Neva Deardorff. Deardorff had known of Butts and his little word game for some while, and might even be considered an early fanatic of the game! She felt that Brunot, a Government administrator and a colleague of hers, might be keen to develop Butts' game further and to market it. Butts and Brunot got together to discuss the possibilities of the game, called Criss-Crosswords by now. Nothing much came of this liaison for some while. Through the war years, Brunot toyed with the idea of turning Criss-Crosswords into a marketable product, while he continued to play the game himself. In 1946, when the war was over, Brunot and Butts came together again. Further discussion and a refinement of certain points resulted in the game being renamed – and Scrabble was born. Butts and Brunot made plans for producing and marketing the game. Finally, in 1949, Scrabble was launched in the USA by Brunot and his Production and Marketing Company in Connecticut, a name which still appears on many Scrabble boards.

However, the game's popularity grew slowly. Total sales for 1949 were just over 2,000 sets, and the company made a loss. 1950 saw almost 5,000 sets sold, but the manufacturer was still losing money. In 1951, sales crept up to 8,500 sets, but the company was scarcely breaking even. Initially, 1952 showed little sign of bringing anything different from the preceding three years. For the first six months sales were nothing special, but in the middle of the year, a watershed was reached. The game suddenly took off with astonishing success. In the next couple of years, Brunot sold 4½ million sets! The USA had gone crazy over Scrabble, just as it was to do a few years later over the hula-hoop and the twist.

The person who had most to do with the transformation of Scrabble from a money-loser into a sure-fire success was a man called Jack Strauss. Strauss was the chairman of Macy's, a very large department store in New York City. He had played Scrabble with some friends during his summer holiday, and when he got back to the store, he was flabbergasted to find that Macy's did not stock the game. Strauss soon changed that, and Macy's was soon running a big promotion for Scrabble. The game took off in the 'Big Apple', and the craze soon spread throughout the country.

Within a year or so, Scrabble was catching on outside the USA. By 1953, it had reached Australia, where it has had a strong hold ever since. The game found its way to Britain in

1954, and has been consistently popular since then. Scrabble has spread to the rest of the English-speaking world and beyond. It has been translated into a variety of foreign languages, including Arabic, Greek and Russian. Scrabble is available in standard sets, de luxe sets, travel sets and pocket sets. It is also obtainable in a number of computer packages which run on several different microcomputers.

In recent years, the game has become much organized. There are Scrabble clubs, inter-club tournaments, regional championships, national championships – even Television Scrabble. There is no *world* championship yet, but to the ardent Scrabble player all things are possible, so it can only be a matter of time!

# 3

# SCRABBLE
# WORD WONDERS

# WHAT IS SCRABBLE?

In an attempt to understand the full meaning of Scrabble, it is useful to consider how different dictionaries define the word 'scrabble'. Only by examining the range of definitions offered will the importance of Scrabble become truly apparent!

Scrabble appears in most dictionaries as a verb and a noun. Only the more modern dictionaries make reference to the game of Scrabble. The definitions of the word 'scrabble' in seven different dictionaries are given here. Notice how they vary slightly from dictionary to dictionary. One definition might refer to scratching with the hands and feet, and another to scraping with claws. One definition might use words like 'grope' and 'search', and another might use 'jostle' and 'struggle'.

*The Concise Oxford Dictionary* (1982 edition)
- to scrawl
- to scribble
- to scratch or grope about to find or collect something
- (with capital, *Registered Trademark*) a game in which players build up words from letter-blocks on a board

*Chambers Twentieth Century Dictionary* (1983 edition)
- to scratch
- to scrape
- to scrawl
- to scramble
- a scrawl
- (with capital, *Registered Trademark*) a word-building game

*The Random House Dictionary of the English Language*
- to scratch or scrape, as with the claws or hands
- to grapple or struggle with or as with the claws or hands
- to scrawl
- to scribble
- to jostle or struggle for possession of something
- to grab or collect something in a disorderly way
- to scramble
- a scratching or scraping, as with the claws or hands
- a scrawled or scribbled writing
- a disorderly struggle for possession of something
- a scramble

- (with capital, *Registered Trademark*) a game combining anagrams and crosswords in which two to four players use counters of various point values to form words on a playing board

*Webster's Third New International Dictionary*
- to scrawl
- to scribble
- to scratch or claw about clumsily or frantically
- to grope or search hastily or blindly
- to struggle for a foothold
- to scramble
- to clamber
- to struggle by or as if by scraping or scratching
- to gather or make hastily by clutching or scraping
- to make scratching movements on
- to mark with irregular lines or letters
- to scribble
- something scribbled or scrawled
- a scribble
- a repeated scratching or clawing
- a scramble
- (with capital) trademark: used for a board game in which players take turns placing letter tiles each with a count value on squares some of which are marked for extra count to form words with as high a count as possible
- of a person, to scramble on hands and feet
- of a person, to stumble or struggle along
- to scratch or make (something) up, off, out, etc., hurriedly
- to obtain by scratching or raking about
- a scrawling character in writing, hence a document composed of such characters
- a picture of or characterized by careless or hastily executed line-work

*A Supplement to the Oxford English Dictionary*
- a scramble
- a confused struggle
- a 'free-for-all'
- the action or sound of scrabbling
- (with capital, *Registered Trademark*) the proprietary name of a game in which players use tiles displaying individual letters to form words on a special board

*Webster's New International Dictionary* (Second edition)
  – to scrape, paw or scratch with the hands or feet
  – to struggle by or as by scraping or scratching with the hands
  – loosely, to work drudgingly
  – to clamber with hands and feet or knees
  – to scramble
  – to scribble
  – to scrawl
  – to gather or make hastily as by scraping or clutching
  – to mark with irregular lines or letters
  – to make scratching movements on or with
  – an act or result of scrabbling
  – a piece of writing carelessly scribbled
  – a scrawl
  – a picture showing careless drawing
  – a scramble

*The Oxford English Dictionary*
  – to make marks at random
  – to write in rambling or scrawling characters
  – to scrawl
  – to scribble
  – to write or depict (something) in a scrawling manner
  – to scrawl upon (something)
  – of an animal, to scratch about hurriedly with the claws or paws
  – of a person, to scratch or scrape about with the hands or feet
  – to make scratching movements with

Even this amazing variety of definitions is by no means complete. Turning to *The English Dialect Dictionary*, edited by Joseph Wright, another whole set of definitions for 'scrabble' can be unearthed. Add all the following to the previous list:

  – to scratch
  – to paw
  – to make clutching movements with the hands
  – to make a scratching noise
  – to scrape up from off the ground
  – to grub about
  – to crawl about on hands and knees
  – to scramble
  – to climb

- to procure with difficulty
- to tease wool
- to scribble
- to scrawl
- to struggle on
- to rub along
- to disagree
- to quarrel
- a scratching
- a scramble
- a contest in gathering things up from the ground on hands and knees
- a scribbling
- a stunted tree or shrub
- thorns and briars
- a thin, shrivelled limb
- a puny, shrivelled person
- a small, scraggy animal

There! Do you now feel that you understand the full import of Scrabble?

A word with such a versatile range of meanings can, of course, be expected to produce offspring, or derivatives. The verb forms SCRABBLED and SCRABBLING are fairly common derivative forms. Dictionaries also show SCRABBLER, one who scrabbles. The word SCRABBLEMENT also exists. It is a noun, meaning writing of a rambling character like that of a madman. Two variant spellings of SCRABBLE are also known. There is SCRABLE, which was a variant spelling of SCRABBLE used in the 17th century; and also the reformed spelling SCRABL. Reformed spellings were popular in the early part of this century, but have faded away completely over the last few decades.

# THE ANAGRAMS OF SCRABBLE

So much of the game of Scrabble is about juggling with letters, trying to make words out of a given set of letters, making anagrams, and so on. The very name of the game itself, SCRABBLE, is not likely to appear often as a word on the Scrabble board. It has eight letters, three of which, the two Bs and the C, are rather awkward.

Even so, it is interesting to see what other words can be formed from the letters of SCRABBLE. A search of a wide variety of dictionaries has unearthed just three anagrams of SCRABBLE. In alphabetical order, they are:

CABBLERS – this is the plural of the noun CABBLER, one who cabbles. Fine, but what does 'cabble' mean? 'To cabble' is to break up iron bars and slabs of iron into pieces suitable for forming into wrought iron. CABBLERS, then, are men who break up chunks of iron in this way. A dying profession, perhaps?

CLABBERS – this is the plural of the noun CLABBER, a word with various meanings. CLABBER is a type of sour milk that has thickened or curdled; it is also mud or mire; and it is one of several card games similar to klaberjass.

SCABBLER – another trade, like the CABBLER. A SCABBLER is a quarryman who shapes stone slabs to make blocks of uniform size and to reduce shipping weight.

You will find CABBLER in *The Oxford English Dictionary*; and CLABBER and SCABBLER in *Webster's Third New International Dictionary*.

If you can find any additional anagrams of SCRABBLE, congratulations!


# WHERE IS SCRABBLE?

In 1950, the town of Hot Springs in the state of New Mexico, USA, changed its name to Truth or Consequences, the name of a popular game of those days. If a town can adopt such a preposterous name and get away with it, surely there ought to be a town somewhere, anywhere, called Scrabble. Is there? Was there ever? And if so, where?

A detailed study of gazetteers and atlases from the past and present has revealed a small town called Scrabble. It is in Rappahannock County, in the state of Virginia, USA. The town is so small that it has no post office, and receives its mail through the nearby towns of Castleton and Woodville. Quite how the town came to be called Scrabble is not known. Was it anything to do with the game?

The search for towns called Scrabble also revealed a place called Scrabbletown, which is in Anne Arundel County, in the state of Maryland, USA. Scrabbletown is just outside another larger town called Mayo. Should you want to write to Scrabbletown, Maryland, its zip code is 21106.

In addition to the towns of Scrabble and Scrabbletown, there exists a tiny village called Hardscrabble, in the state of New York, USA. This is surely a reference to the hard life led by the early dwellers there, and not to any difficulties they may have with playing the game of Scrabble!

Do you know of any other Scrabble towns, rivers, mountains, etc. anywhere at all in the world? The USA and Australia would seem to be the best countries on which to concentrate an even more detailed search.


# IT'S NEAR


What, you may ask, is near? Christmas, the year 2001, or what? The letters of the phrase 'it's near', AEINRST, always bring a gleam to a Scrabbler's eye. They are regarded as the most anagrammable set of seven letters, and should usually enable a player to place a bonus word somewhere on the board, unless the end of the game is close or the board is extremely tightly-packed with words that cannot be extended. Nine times out of ten, though, the Scrabbler should be able to get down his seven letters, either making a seven-letter word or combining them with a letter already on the board to make an eight-letter word. What are the anagrams of AEINRST? Well, it depends on which dictionary you choose as your authority. The 1983 *Chambers* has nine anagrams of AEINRST:

| | | |
|---|---|---|
| NASTIER | RETAINS | STAINER |
| RATINES | RETINAS | STARNIE |
| RESIANT | RETSINA | STEARIN |

*The Official Scrabble Players Dictionary* has seven of these nine, omitting RESIANT and STARNIE, but has the additional ANESTRI. That's ten anagrams from just two dictionaries. In the bigger, unabridged dictionaries a whole host of other AEINRST anagrams can be found. These include ANTSIER, ASTERIN, ERANIST, ESTRAIN, NERITAS, RANITES, RANTIES, RANTISE, RESTAIN, SERTAIN, STRAINE, TANIERS, TIRANES and TRAINES.

23

What about eight-letter words which can be made from AEINRST plus a letter already on the board? At least 20 of the 26 letters of the alphabet can be combined with AEINRST:

| | | | | | |
|---|---|---|---|---|---|
| +A | ANTISERA | +H | INEARTHS | +P | PANTRIES |
| +B | BANISTER | +I | INERTIAS | +R | STRAINER |
| +C | CANISTER | +K | KERATINS | +S | STAINERS |
| +D | STRAINED | +L | ENTRAILS | +T | NITRATES |
| +E | TRAINEES | +M | MINARETS | +U | URINATES |
| +F | FAINTERS | +N | ENTRAINS | +W | TINWARES |
| +G | GRANITES | +O | NOTARIES | | |

There are plenty of others, like SCANTIER, LATRINES, RAIMENTS, STRAITEN and so on.

# IS YOUR NAME A VALID SCRABBLE WORD?

*'Any words found in a standard dictionary are permitted, except those starting with a capital letter . . .'*

That's what the official Scrabble rules say. And yet there are hundreds of words normally thought of as taking a capital letter which can also be spelled without an initial capital. Names of months, names of countries, towns, and rivers, forenames – these are just a few of the groups which might seem to be invalid for Scrabble, and yet which can offer many words which are allowable.

Take forenames, for example. Here is a list of 100 forenames, all of which can be used in Scrabble. All of these words have other meanings and can be spelled with a lower-case initial letter, according to the 1983 edition of *Chambers Twentieth Century Dictionary*. Out of interest, how many of these 100 can you define?

| | | | |
|---|---|---|---|
| ABIGAIL | BETTY | DICK | FAY |
| ALBERT | BILL | DICKENS | FELICITY |
| ALMA | BOB | DICKY | FLORA |
| ANN | CAROL | DOLLY | FRANK |
| ANNA | CICELY | DON | GRACE |
| BASIL | CLEMENT | EMMA | HANK |
| BEN | COLIN | ERIC | HAZEL |
| BERTHA | CRAIG | FAITH | HEATHER |
| BERYL | DAN | FANNY | HENRY |

| IRIS | KEN | OLIVE | SALLY |
| IVY | KIRK | OLIVER | SAM |
| JACK | LAURA | OTTO | SAUL |
| JAKE | LOUIS | PANSY | SOPHIA |
| JAMES | LUKE | PATRICK | TAFFY |
| JANE | MADGE | PATTY | TED |
| JEAN | MARIA | PAUL | TEDDY |
| JEFF | MARK | PEGGY | TERRY |
| JERRY | MARTIN | PETER | TIMOTHY |
| JESS | MATT | PHOEBE | TOBY |
| JILL | MONA | POLLY | TOMMY |
| JO | MUNGO | ROB | TONY |
| JOCK | NED | ROBIN | VICTOR |
| JOE | NELLY | ROSE | WALLY |
| JOHN | NICK | RUBY | WATT |
| JOSH | NORMA | RUTH | WILLY |

There was a film made at the end of the 1960s called *Bob and Carol and Ted and Alice*. Most filmgoers could be forgiven for thinking that these were the names of the four main characters in the film. To the trained eye of a Scrabble player, the name of the film is a list of three allowable Scrabble words (BOB, CAROL and TED). Quite where Alice fits in is a mystery. No dictionary at all lists the word ALICE with a lower-case initial letter. Perhaps the film would have been better named *Bob and Carol and Ted and Alma*!

# THE PLACENAMES OF CANADA

Take any country in which English is widely used or is the main language, be it the USA, Scotland, Canada, or even England itself. The chances are that many of the placenames on a map of that country will be valid Scrabble words. The USA has BUFFALO, FLINT, MOBILE and PHOENIX; Scotland has BOWLING, DOLLAR, MAIDENS and WICK; and England has BATH, DEAL, HULL and WELLS. Of course, there are lots more than just these few.

Just to show that these are only the tip of the proverbial iceberg, take a detailed map of Canada. Pore over it, and you will find dozens of placenames which are also Scrabble words. Here is a list of nearly 100 Canadian placenames which are also genuine Scrabble words, according to the 1983 edition of *Chambers*.

## Alberta
BROOKS, CORONATION, EMPRESS, HYTHE, JASPER, OLDS, PIBROCH, SMITH, VULCAN, WATERWAYS

## British Columbia
BEND, HOPE, NELSON, OLIVER, PACIFIC, PALLING, PREMIER, TERRACE, TRAIL, VICTORIA

## Manitoba
BADGER, BARROWS, DAUPHIN, DECIMAL, LAMPREY, MAGNET, PINEY, POPE, SNOWFLAKE, VISTA

## New Brunswick
ALBERT, ALMA, BATH, JUNIPER, PEEL

## Newfoundland
BRANCH, CARTWRIGHT, CHANNEL, GANDER, MOBILE, MOSQUITO, NAIN, RENEWS, SALVAGE, VICTORIA

## Nova Scotia
CANNING, DOMINION, ECONOMY, GORE, PROSPECT

## Northwest Territories
RELIANCE, SNOWDRIFT

## Ontario
ACTON, ALMA, COBALT, FLETCHER, FOREST, MARATHON, MIDLAND, MOONBEAM, SULTAN, TWEED

## Prince Edward Island
CARDIGAN, PORTAGE, VICTORIA

## Quebec
ANGERS, ASBESTOS, BURY, CARRIER, CEDARS, FOSTER, MAGPIE, PARENT, PERKINS, WEIR

## Saskatchewan
CLIMAX, CONSUL, ELBOW, LEADER, MILESTONE, OUTLOOK, PRELATE, REGINA, ROULEAU, UNITY

## Yukon
CHAMPAGNE, SNAG

So what, you might ask. What's the point of knowing that various placenames are legal words in Scrabble? Well, it's just another way of cementing in your mind that various sequences of letters can be used in the game of Scrabble. For example, who knows when you may next need to play the eight-letter word VICTORIA? Until now, you may have been unaware that it could be used in Scrabble. But you now know that it doesn't have to begin with a capital letter!

## U AFTER Q EXCEPT . . .

One of the most enduring pieces of orthographic folklore is the assertion that the letter Q is always followed by the letter U. This is usually the view of the tyro Scrabble player. But give him a few games with an experienced Scrabble player, and he will soon change his mind. You see, there are a considerable number of words in which Q is not followed by U, and which can be found in English-language dictionaries. Many of these words do indeed originate from foreign parts, but dictionary editors have recognized their absorption into the English language and have therefore included them in their dictionaries.

A quick check of *The Official Scrabble Players Dictionary* reveals five words beginning with a Q not followed by a U: QAID, QINDAR, QINTAR, QIVIUT and QOPH. All of these are nouns to which an S is added to form the plural. That's ten different words already.

A similar check of the 1983 edition of *Chambers Twentieth Century Dictionary* yields five words beginning with a Q not followed by a U, only one of them being in *The Official Scrabble Players Dictionary*'s list: QADI, QALAMDAN, QANAT, QIBLA and QINTAR. Plural forms are generated by the straightforward addition of an S in all these cases.

Both of these dictionaries also give words which contain Q (not as the initial letter) not followed by a U. *The Official Scrabble Players Dictionary* has FAQIR, for example, and *Chambers* has BURQA, INQILAB and SUQ.

By searching through a variety of different dictionaries, it is possible to build up a list of Q-not-followed-by-U words. Using just a half dozen dictionaries, the collection of 74 words given here was put together. The dictionaries that were trawled for these 74 words were: the 1983 edition of *Chambers Twentieth Century Dictionary*, *Webster's New International Dictionary* (Second Edition), *Webster's Third New International Dictionary*, *The Random House Dictionary*, *Funk and Wagnalls New Standard Dictionary* and *The Oxford English Dictionary* and its various supplements. A very large number of obsolete words from the *Oxford* have been excluded as they involve the substitution of W for U (for example, SQWARE for SQUARE) or the substitution of QW for WH (as in QWERE for WHERE).

This list of words was built up by Dmitri Borgmann, Ross Eckler, Homer Calkins and Philip Cohen, all of the USA, and Darryl Francis, of Surrey, England. A shorter, less complete version of this list appeared in the May 1976 edition of *Word Ways*, The Journal of Recreational Linguistics.

BATHQOL – a divine revelation in Hebrew tradition
BURQA – a veiled garment worn by Moslem women
CINQ – the number five in dice or cards
CINQFOIL – a plant of the genus Potentilla
COQ – a trimming of cock feathers on a woman's hat
FAQIH – a Moslem theologian
FAQIR – a Moslem mendicant or ascetic
FIQH – Moslem jurisprudence based on theology
FUQAHA – the plural of FAQIH
INQILAB – in India, Pakistan, etc., revolution
MIQRA – the Hebrew text of the Bible
MUQADDAM – a head-man
NASTALIQ – an Arabic script used in Persian poetical writings
PAQ – a South American rodent
QABAB – another spelling of KEBAB, pieces of meat roasted on
  a skewer
QABBALA – a mystical interpretation of the Bible
QABBALAH – same as QABBALA
QADHI – same as QADI
QADI – a Moslem judge dealing in religious law
QAF – the 21st letter of the Arabic alphabet
QAID – a local official in Spain or North Africa
QAIMAQAM – a minor official of the Ottoman Empire
QAIMMAQAM – same as QAIMAQAM
QALAMDAN – a Persian writing-case
QANAT – an underground channel
QANEH – an ancient Hebrew measure of length
QANON – a type of dulcimer, harp or sackbut
QANTAR – a Mediterranean unit of weight
QANUN – same as QANON
QASAB – an ancient Near East unit of length
QASABA – an ancient Arabian measure of area
QASIDA – a laudatory or satiric Arabian poem
QAT – an Arabian shrub used as a narcotic
QAZI – same as QADI
QERE – a marginal reading in the Hebrew Bible
QERI – same as QERE

QI – physical life force postulated by certain Chinese philosophers

QIANA – nylon

QIBLA – the point toward which Moslems turn in prayer

QIBLAH – same as QIBLA

QIBLI – a local name in Libya for the sirocco (a hot, dusty wind)

QINAH – a Hebrew elegy

QINDAR – same as QINTAR

QINOT – the plural of QINAH

QINOTH – same as QINOT

QINTAR – an Albanian unit of money

QIVIUT – the wool of the undercoat of the musk-ox

QIYAS – analogical interpretation of Moslem law

QOBAR – a dry fog of the Upper Nile

QOPH – the 19th letter of the Hebrew alphabet

QRE – same as QERE

QRI – same as QERE

QS – the plural of the letter Q

QT – quiet; usually used in the phrase 'on the qt'

QVINT – a Danish weight

QVINTIN – same as QVINT

SAMBUQ – a small Arabian boat

SHOQ – an East Indian tree

SHURQEE – a south-easterly wind of the Persian Gulf

SUQ – a market-place in the Moslem world

TALUQ – an Indian estate including subtenants

TALUQDAR – a collector of the taluq's revenues

TALUQDARI – a landholding tenure in India

TAQIYA – outward Moslem conformity in a hostile environment

TAQIYAH – same as TAQIYA

TAQLID – uncritical acceptance of a Moslem orthodoxy

TARIQA – mystical communion

TARIQAH – same as TARIQA

TARIQAT – same as TARIQA

TRINQ – an oracular statement in Rabelais' *Pantagruel*

WAQF – a charitable trust in Moslem law

YAQONA – an intoxicating beverage

ZAQQUM – a tree with bitter fruit, mentioned in the Koran

ZINDIQ – a heretic extremely unfaithful to Islam

This list is not offered with the recommendation, or even suggestion, that you should adopt such words in your normal Scrabble play. It is put forward to demonstrate that each dictionary has its own small collection of Q-not-followed-by-U words, and any serious Scrabble player should know those words which appear in his or her own dictionary of authority.

# TWO-LETTER WORDS

The proper use of two-letter words in Scrabble cannot be stressed too strongly. There are many Scrabble players who believe that the rules of the game forbid two-letter words. This is not so. Two-letter words are perfectly permissible in Scrabble, as long as they conform with all the usual rules of acceptability. Two-letter words are important because they allow the player to make other words at the same time. Consider the example on page 31. The words CAT, WHELP, CHECK and PUT are already on the board. Your turn is next, and the seven tiles on your rack are CEIPRTU. Can you make a seven-letter word from these tiles? If so, is there anywhere to put it on the board? You ought to be able to spot PICTURE, and you might know that CUPRITE is a word, too. Will either of them go down on the board? There are two possibilities, and they both involve the use of two-letter words. First of all, you could play PICTURE, above and parallel to CAT, making the two-letter words PA and IT at the same time. Secondly, you could play PICTURE, to the right of and parallel to PUT, making the two-letter words UP and TI in the process. These two moves score 78 and 74 points respectively. Two-letter words are very often used in this way to assist in the positioning of seven-letter words.

Novice players tend to stick to the everyday two-letter words such as AT, GO, IF and ON. But experienced players can make use of the full range of two-letter words in the dictionary they are using as their authority.

The two-letter words that appear in different dictionaries vary tremendously. The total number of such words is usually in direct proportion to the size of the dictionary. Some words which have only come into wide use in the past few years tend to be excluded from the dictionaries of 20 or 30 years ago.

Just to demonstrate how much variation there is in the number of two-letter words offered by dictionaries, the charts on the next few pages have been put together. These charts list all the two-letter words which appear in 11 major dictionaries. (Full details of all the dictionaries are given in the bibliography.) There is a total of 230 two-letter words in this compilation, and yet the numbers in individual dictionaries vary from 71 (not quite a third of the total) to 189 (just over 80 per cent).

A few points should be noted when referring to the charts. A tick in a particular column means that the corresponding word appears in the dictionary listed at the head of the column. The letter O is used to indicate that a word is in the dictionary concerned, but is marked as obsolete. The letter R is used to

C A T

C H E C K

W H E L P

P U T

indicate that a word is in the relevant dictionary, but is a so-called reformed spelling. Plural forms (such as BS, CS, DS and so on) are only marked with a tick if they are specifically listed as such in the dictionary.

The use of all of these words, or even of certain of them, is not necessarily being advocated. The Scrabble player should select his or her own dictionary, and stick to it during a game.

| | Chambers Twentieth Century Dictionary (1972 edition) | Chambers Twentieth Century Dictionary (1983 edition) | Collins English Dictionary | Concise Oxford Dictionary (1982 edition) | Funk and Wagnalls New Standard Dictionary (1946 edition) | Oxford English Dictionary and its Supplements | Official Scrabble Players Dictionary | Random House Dictionary | Webster's New Collegiate Dictionary (Eighth edition) | Webster's New International Dictionary (Second edition) | Webster's Third New International Dictionary |
|---|---|---|---|---|---|---|---|---|---|---|---|
| aa | | | ✓ | | ✓ | ✓ | ✓ | ✓ | | ✓ | ✓ |
| ab | | | | | | O | | | | | ✓ |
| ac | | | | | | O | | | | O | |
| ad | ✓ | ✓ | ✓ | ✓ | ✓ | O | ✓ | ✓ | ✓ | ✓ | ✓ |
| ae | ✓ | ✓ | ✓ | | ✓ | ✓ | ✓ | ✓ | ✓ | ✓ | ✓ |
| af | | | | | | ✓ | | | | | |
| ag | | | | | | | | | | | ✓ |
| ah | ✓ | ✓ | ✓ | ✓ | ✓ | ✓ | ✓ | ✓ | ✓ | ✓ | ✓ |
| ai | ✓ | ✓ | ✓ | ✓ | ✓ | ✓ | ✓ | ✓ | ✓ | ✓ | ✓ |
| ak | | | | | ✓ | ✓ | | | | ✓ | |
| al | | | | | ✓ | O | | | | ✓ | ✓ |
| am | ✓ | ✓ | ✓ | ✓ | ✓ | ✓ | ✓ | ✓ | ✓ | ✓ | ✓ |
| an | ✓ | ✓ | ✓ | ✓ | ✓ | ✓ | ✓ | ✓ | ✓ | ✓ | ✓ |
| ar | ✓ | ✓ | | | ✓ | ✓ | ✓ | | ✓ | ✓ | ✓ |
| as | ✓ | ✓ | ✓ | ✓ | ✓ | ✓ | ✓ | ✓ | ✓ | ✓ | ✓ |
| at | ✓ | ✓ | ✓ | ✓ | ✓ | ✓ | ✓ | ✓ | ✓ | ✓ | ✓ |
| au | | | | | ✓ | O | | ✓ | | ✓ | |
| av | | | | | | | | | | | ✓ |

| | Chambers Twentieth Century Dictionary (1972 edition) | Chambers Twentieth Century Dictionary (1983 edition) | Collins English Dictionary | Concise Oxford Dictionary (1982 edition) | Funk and Wagnalls New Standard Dictionary (1946 edition) | Oxford English Dictionary and its Supplements | Official Scrabble Players Dictionary | Random House Dictionary | Webster's New Collegiate Dictionary (Eighth edition) | Webster's New International Dictionary (Second edition) | Webster's Third New International Dictionary |
|---|---|---|---|---|---|---|---|---|---|---|---|
| aw | | ✓ | ✓ | ✓ | O | ✓ | ✓ | ✓ | ✓ | ✓ | ✓ |
| ax | ✓ | ✓ | ✓ | ✓ | ✓ | ✓ | ✓ | ✓ | ✓ | ✓ | ✓ |
| ay | ✓ | ✓ | ✓ | ✓ | ✓ | ✓ | ✓ | ✓ | ✓ | ✓ | ✓ |
| ba | | | | | ✓ | O | ✓ | ✓ | ✓ | ✓ | ✓ |
| bb | | | | | | | | | | | ✓ |
| be | ✓ | ✓ | ✓ | ✓ | ✓ | ✓ | ✓ | ✓ | ✓ | ✓ | ✓ |
| bi | | | | | | ✓ | ✓ | | ✓ | | |
| bo | ✓ | ✓ | ✓ | ✓ | ✓ | ✓ | ✓ | | | ✓ | ✓ |
| bs | | | | | | | | ✓ | ✓ | ✓ | ✓ |
| bu | | | | | | ✓ | | | | ✓ | ✓ |
| by | ✓ | ✓ | ✓ | ✓ | ✓ | ✓ | ✓ | ✓ | ✓ | ✓ | ✓ |
| ca | | | | | ✓ | ✓ | | | | | |
| ce | | | | | | ✓ | | | | ✓ | ✓ |
| ch | O | O | | | | O | | | | O | |
| co | | | | | | ✓ | | | | O | |
| cs | | | | | | | | ✓ | ✓ | ✓ | ✓ |
| cu | | | | | | O | | | | | |
| cy | | | | | | ✓ | | | | | |

| | Chambers Twentieth Century Dictionary (1972 edition) | Chambers Twentieth Century Dictionary (1983 edition) | Collins English Dictionary | Concise Oxford Dictionary (1982 edition) | Funk and Wagnalls New Standard Dictionary (1946 edition) | Oxford English Dictionary and its Supplements | Official Scrabble Players Dictionary | Random House Dictionary | Webster's New Collegiate Dictionary (Eighth edition) | Webster's New International Dictionary (Second edition) | Webster's Third New International Dictionary |
|----|----|----|----|----|----|----|----|----|----|----|----|
| da | ✓ | ✓ | | | ✓ | ✓ | ✓ | | | ✓ | ✓ |
| de | | | ✓ | | ✓ | ✓ | ✓ | ✓ | | ✓ | ✓ |
| di | | | | | | | | ✓ | | ✓ | |
| do | ✓ | ✓ | ✓ | ✓ | ✓ | ✓ | ✓ | ✓ | ✓ | ✓ | ✓ |
| ds | | | | | | | | ✓ | ✓ | ✓ | ✓ |
| du | | | | | | ✓ | | ✓ | | ✓ | ✓ |
| dy | | | | ✓ | | ✓ | | | | | |
| ea | ✓ | ✓ | | | ✓ | ✓ | | | | ✓ | ✓ |
| eb | | | | | R | | | | | R | |
| ed | | | | | | O | | | | | |
| ee | ✓ | ✓ | | | ✓ | ✓ | | | | ✓ | ✓ |
| ef | ✓ | ✓ | | | | ✓ | ✓ | | ✓ | ✓ | ✓ |
| eg | | | | | R | | | | | RO | |
| eh | ✓ | ✓ | ✓ | ✓ | ✓ | ✓ | ✓ | ✓ | ✓ | ✓ | ✓ |
| ei | | | | | ✓ | ✓ | | | | | |
| el | ✓ | ✓ | ✓ | ✓ | ✓ | O | ✓ | ✓ | ✓ | ✓ | ✓ |
| em | ✓ | ✓ | ✓ | ✓ | ✓ | ✓ | ✓ | ✓ | ✓ | ✓ | ✓ |
| en | ✓ | ✓ | ✓ | ✓ | ✓ | ✓ | ✓ | ✓ | ✓ | ✓ | ✓ |

| | Chambers Twentieth Century Dictionary (1972 edition) | Chambers Twentieth Century Dictionary (1983 edition) | Collins English Dictionary | Concise Oxford Dictionary (1982 edition) | Funk and Wagnalls New Standard Dictionary (1946 edition) | Oxford English Dictionary and its Supplements | Official Scrabble Players Dictionary | Random House Dictionary | Webster's New Collegiate Dictionary (Eighth edition) | Webster's New International Dictionary (Second edition) | Webster's Third New International Dictionary |
|---|---|---|---|---|---|---|---|---|---|---|---|
| er | ✓ | ✓ | ✓ | ✓ | R | O | ✓ | ✓ | | ✓ | ✓ |
| es | ✓ | ✓ | | | | O | ✓ | ✓ | ✓ | ✓ | ✓ |
| et | | | | | | ✓ | ✓ | ✓ | ✓ | ✓ | ✓ |
| eu | | | | | | O | | | | ✓ | |
| ew | | | | | O | O | | | | O | |
| ex | ✓ | ✓ | ✓ | ✓ | ✓ | ✓ | ✓ | ✓ | ✓ | ✓ | ✓ |
| ey | | | | | R | O | | | | ✓ | |
| fa | ✓ | ✓ | ✓ | ✓ | ✓ | ✓ | ✓ | ✓ | ✓ | ✓ | ✓ |
| fe | | | | | ✓ | O | | | | ✓ | |
| fi | | | | | | | | ✓ | | ✓ | |
| fo | | | | | O | O | | | | O | |
| fs | | | | | | | | ✓ | ✓ | ✓ | ✓ |
| fu | | | | | ✓ | | | | | ✓ | |
| fy | ✓ | ✓ | | | ✓ | O | | | | | |
| ga | | | | | | ✓ | | | | ✓ | ✓ |
| ge | | | | | | | | | | ✓ | ✓ |
| gi | | ✓ | | | | | | | | | ✓ |
| go | ✓ | ✓ | ✓ | ✓ | ✓ | ✓ | ✓ | ✓ | ✓ | ✓ | ✓ |

| | Chambers Twentieth Century Dictionary (1972 edition) | Chambers Twentieth Century Dictionary (1983 edition) | Collins English Dictionary | Concise Oxford Dictionary (1982 edition) | Funk and Wagnalls New Standard Dictionary (1946 edition) | Oxford English Dictionary and its Supplements | Official Scrabble Players Dictionary | Random House Dictionary | Webster's New Collegiate Dictionary (Eighth edition) | Webster's New International Dictionary (Second edition) | Webster's Third New International Dictionary |
|----|----|----|----|----|----|----|----|----|----|----|----|
| gs | | | | | | | | ✓ | ✓ | ✓ | ✓ |
| gu | ✓ | ✓ | | | | | | | | | |
| gy | | | | | | O | | | | | |
| ha | ✓ | ✓ | ✓ | ✓ | ✓ | ✓ | ✓ | ✓ | ✓ | ✓ | ✓ |
| he | ✓ | ✓ | ✓ | ✓ | ✓ | ✓ | ✓ | ✓ | ✓ | ✓ | ✓ |
| hi | ✓ | ✓ | ✓ | ✓ | ✓ | ✓ | ✓ | ✓ | ✓ | ✓ | ✓ |
| hm | | | | | | ✓ | | | | ✓ | |
| ho | ✓ | ✓ | | ✓ | ✓ | ✓ | ✓ | ✓ | ✓ | ✓ | ✓ |
| hs | | | | | | | | ✓ | ✓ | ✓ | ✓ |
| hu | | | | | | O | | | | ✓ | ✓ |
| hw | | | | | | ✓ | | | | | |
| hy | | | | | O | ✓ | | | | O | |
| id | ✓ | ✓ | ✓ | ✓ | ✓ | ✓ | ✓ | ✓ | ✓ | ✓ | ✓ |
| ie | | | | ✓ | | | | | | ✓ | ✓ |
| if | ✓ | ✓ | ✓ | ✓ | ✓ | ✓ | ✓ | ✓ | ✓ | ✓ | ✓ |
| ik | | | | | | ✓ | | | | | |
| il | | | | | | O | | | | R | |
| im | | | | | | O | | | | | |

| | Chambers Twentieth Century Dictionary (1972 edition) | Chambers Twentieth Century Dictionary (1983 edition) | Collins English Dictionary | Concise Oxford Dictionary (1982 edition) | Funk and Wagnalls New Standard Dictionary (1946 edition) | Oxford English Dictionary and its Supplements | Official Scrabble Players Dictionary | Random House Dictionary | Webster's New Collegiate Dictionary (Eighth edition) | Webster's New International Dictionary (Second edition) | Webster's Third New International Dictionary |
|---|---|---|---|---|---|---|---|---|---|---|---|
| in | ✓ | ✓ | ✓ | ✓ | ✓ | ✓ | ✓ | ✓ | ✓ | ✓ | ✓ |
| io | ✓ | ✓ | | | ✓ | ✓ | | | | ✓ | ✓ |
| ir | | | | | | O | | | | | |
| is | ✓ | ✓ | ✓ | ✓ | ✓ | ✓ | ✓ | ✓ | ✓ | ✓ | ✓ |
| it | ✓ | ✓ | ✓ | ✓ | ✓ | ✓ | ✓ | ✓ | ✓ | ✓ | ✓ |
| iw | | | | | | O | | | | | |
| ja | | | | | | O | | ✓ | | ✓ | |
| jo | ✓ | ✓ | ✓ | ✓ | ✓ | ✓ | ✓ | ✓ | ✓ | ✓ | ✓ |
| js | | | | | | | | ✓ | ✓ | ✓ | ✓ |
| ka | ✓ | ✓ | ✓ | | ✓ | ✓ | ✓ | ✓ | | ✓ | ✓ |
| ki | | | | | | ✓ | | | | ✓ | ✓ |
| ko | | | | | | ✓ | | | | ✓ | ✓ |
| ks | | | | | | | | ✓ | ✓ | ✓ | ✓ |
| ku | | | | | | O | | | | | |
| ky | ✓ | ✓ | | | | ✓ | | | | | |
| la | ✓ | ✓ | ✓ | ✓ | ✓ | ✓ | ✓ | ✓ | ✓ | ✓ | ✓ |
| le | | | | | ✓ | O | | | | ✓ | |
| li | ✓ | ✓ | ✓ | ✓ | ✓ | ✓ | ✓ | ✓ | ✓ | ✓ | ✓ |

| | Chambers Twentieth Century Dictionary (1972 edition) | Chambers Twentieth Century Dictionary (1983 edition) | Collins English Dictionary | Concise Oxford Dictionary (1982 edition) | Funk and Wagnalls New Standard Dictionary (1946 edition) | Oxford English Dictionary and its Supplements | Official Scrabble Players Dictionary | Random House Dictionary | Webster's New Collegiate Dictionary (Eighth edition) | Webster's New International Dictionary (Second edition) | Webster's Third New International Dictionary |
|---|---|---|---|---|---|---|---|---|---|---|---|
| lo | ✓ | ✓ | ✓ | ✓ | ✓ | ✓ | ✓ | ✓ | ✓ | ✓ | ✓ |
| ls | | | | | | | | ✓ | ✓ | ✓ | ✓ |
| lu | | | | | ✓ | O | | | | | ✓ |
| ly | | | | | | ✓ | | | | ✓ | |
| ma | ✓ | ✓ | ✓ | ✓ | ✓ | ✓ | ✓ | ✓ | ✓ | ✓ | ✓ |
| me | ✓ | ✓ | ✓ | ✓ | ✓ | ✓ | ✓ | ✓ | ✓ | ✓ | ✓ |
| mi | ✓ | ✓ | ✓ | ✓ | ✓ | ✓ | ✓ | ✓ | ✓ | ✓ | ✓ |
| mo | ✓ | ✓ | ✓ | ✓ | ✓ | ✓ | ✓ | ✓ | | ✓ | ✓ |
| ms | | | | | | | | ✓ | ✓ | ✓ | ✓ |
| mu | ✓ | ✓ | ✓ | ✓ | ✓ | ✓ | ✓ | ✓ | ✓ | ✓ | ✓ |
| my | ✓ | ✓ | ✓ | ✓ | ✓ | ✓ | ✓ | ✓ | ✓ | ✓ | ✓ |
| na | ✓ | ✓ | | ✓ | ✓ | ✓ | ✓ | ✓ | | ✓ | ✓ |
| ne | O | O | | ✓ | ✓ | ✓ | | | | ✓ | ✓ |
| ni | | | | | | O | | | | ✓ | |
| no | ✓ | ✓ | ✓ | ✓ | ✓ | ✓ | ✓ | ✓ | ✓ | ✓ | ✓ |
| ns | | | | | | | | ✓ | ✓ | ✓ | ✓ |
| nu | ✓ | ✓ | ✓ | ✓ | ✓ | ✓ | ✓ | ✓ | | ✓ | ✓ |
| ny | O | O | | | O | ✓ | | | | O | |

| | Chambers Twentieth Century Dictionary (1972 edition) | Chambers Twentieth Century Dictionary (1983 edition) | Collins English Dictionary | Concise Oxford Dictionary (1982 edition) | Funk and Wagnalls New Standard Dictionary (1946 edition) | Oxford English Dictionary and its Supplements | Official Scrabble Players Dictionary | Random House Dictionary | Webster's New Collegiate Dictionary (Eighth edition) | Webster's New International Dictionary (Second edition) | Webster's Third New International Dictionary |
|---|---|---|---|---|---|---|---|---|---|---|---|
| ob | ✓ | ✓ | | | O | ✓ | | ✓ | | O | |
| oc | | | | | | ✓ | | | | ✓ | |
| od | ✓ | ✓ | ✓ | ✓ | ✓ | ✓ | ✓ | ✓ | ✓ | ✓ | ✓ |
| oe | ✓ | ✓ | | | ✓ | ✓ | ✓ | ✓ | | ✓ | ✓ |
| of | ✓ | ✓ | ✓ | ✓ | ✓ | ✓ | ✓ | ✓ | ✓ | ✓ | ✓ |
| og | | | | | | O | | | | | |
| oh | ✓ | ✓ | ✓ | ✓ | ✓ | ✓ | ✓ | ✓ | ✓ | ✓ | ✓ |
| oi | | ✓ | | | | ✓ | | ✓ | | | |
| ok | | | | | | ✓ | | | | O | |
| ol | | | | | | ✓ | | | | | |
| om | | | | | | ✓ | ✓ | | ✓ | ✓ | ✓ |
| on | ✓ | ✓ | ✓ | ✓ | ✓ | ✓ | ✓ | ✓ | ✓ | ✓ | ✓ |
| oo | ✓ | ✓ | | | ✓ | ✓ | | | | ✓ | ✓ |
| op | | ✓ | | ✓ | | ✓ | ✓ | | | | ✓ |
| or | ✓ | ✓ | ✓ | ✓ | ✓ | ✓ | ✓ | ✓ | ✓ | ✓ | ✓ |
| os | ✓ | ✓ | ✓ | | ✓ | ✓ | ✓ | ✓ | ✓ | ✓ | ✓ |
| ou | ✓ | ✓ | | | | ✓ | | | | ✓ | ✓ |
| ow | ✓ | ✓ | ✓ | ✓ | ✓ | ✓ | ✓ | ✓ | | ✓ | ✓ |

| | Chambers Twentieth Century Dictionary (1972 edition) | Chambers Twentieth Century Dictionary (1983 edition) | Collins English Dictionary | Concise Oxford Dictionary (1982 edition) | Funk and Wagnalls New Standard Dictionary (1946 edition) | Oxford English Dictionary and its Supplements | Official Scrabble Players Dictionary | Random House Dictionary | Webster's New Collegiate Dictionary (Eighth edition) | Webster's New International Dictionary (Second edition) | Webster's Third New International Dictionary |
|---|---|---|---|---|---|---|---|---|---|---|---|
| ox | ✓ | ✓ | ✓ | ✓ | ✓ | ✓ | ✓ | ✓ | ✓ | ✓ | ✓ |
| oy | ✓ | ✓ | | | ✓ | ✓ | ✓ | ✓ | | ✓ | ✓ |
| pa | ✓ | ✓ | ✓ | ✓ | ✓ | ✓ | ✓ | ✓ | ✓ | ✓ | ✓ |
| pe | | | ✓ | | ✓ | O | ✓ | ✓ | ✓ | ✓ | ✓ |
| pi | ✓ | ✓ | ✓ | ✓ | ✓ | ✓ | ✓ | ✓ | ✓ | ✓ | ✓ |
| po | | ✓ | ✓ | ✓ | ✓ | ✓ | | | | ✓ | |
| ps | | | | | | | | ✓ | ✓ | ✓ | ✓ |
| pu | | | | | ✓ | ✓ | | | | ✓ | ✓ |
| py | | | | | | O | | | | O | |
| qi | | | | | | ✓ | | | | | |
| qs | | | | | | | | ✓ | ✓ | ✓ | ✓ |
| qt | | | | | | | | | ✓ | | ✓ |
| qu | | | | | O | O | | | | O | |
| ra | | | | | | ✓ | | ✓ | | ✓ | |
| re | ✓ | ✓ | ✓ | ✓ | ✓ | ✓ | ✓ | ✓ | ✓ | ✓ | ✓ |
| ri | | | | | | ✓ | | | | ✓ | ✓ |
| ro | | | | | | O | | | | ✓ | ✓ |
| rs | | | | | | | | ✓ | ✓ | ✓ | ✓ |

| | Chambers Twentieth Century Dictionary (1972 edition) | Chambers Twentieth Century Dictionary (1983 edition) | Collins English Dictionary | Concise Oxford Dictionary (1982 edition) | Funk and Wagnalls New Standard Dictionary (1946 edition) | Oxford English Dictionary and its Supplements | Official Scrabble Players Dictionary | Random House Dictionary | Webster's New Collegiate Dictionary (Eighth edition) | Webster's New International Dictionary (Second edition) | Webster's Third New International Dictionary |
|---|---|---|---|---|---|---|---|---|---|---|---|
| ru | | | | | | O | | | | ✓ | |
| sa | | | | | | | | | | ✓ | ✓ |
| se | | | | | | O | | | | ✓ | |
| sh | ✓ | ✓ | ✓ | ✓ | ✓ | ✓ | ✓ | | ✓ | ✓ | ✓ |
| si | ✓ | ✓ | ✓ | ✓ | ✓ | ✓ | ✓ | ✓ | ✓ | ✓ | ✓ |
| so | ✓ | ✓ | ✓ | ✓ | ✓ | ✓ | ✓ | ✓ | ✓ | ✓ | ✓ |
| ss | | | | | | | | ✓ | ✓ | ✓ | ✓ |
| st | ✓ | ✓ | | | | ✓ | | | | ✓ | |
| su | | | | | | ✓ | | | | | |
| sy | | | | | ✓ | O | | | | ✓ | ✓ |
| ta | ✓ | ✓ | ✓ | ✓ | | ✓ | ✓ | ✓ | ✓ | ✓ | ✓ |
| te | ✓ | ✓ | ✓ | ✓ | | ✓ | | ✓ | | ✓ | ✓ |
| ti | ✓ | ✓ | ✓ | ✓ | ✓ | ✓ | ✓ | ✓ | ✓ | ✓ | ✓ |
| to | ✓ | ✓ | ✓ | ✓ | ✓ | ✓ | ✓ | ✓ | ✓ | ✓ | ✓ |
| ts | | | | | | | | ✓ | ✓ | ✓ | ✓ |
| tu | | | | | | O | | | | ✓ | |
| tv | | | | | | | | | ✓ | | |
| ty | | | | | | O | | | | ✓ | |

| | Chambers Twentieth Century Dictionary (1972 edition) | Chambers Twentieth Century Dictionary (1983 edition) | Collins English Dictionary | Concise Oxford Dictionary (1982 edition) | Funk and Wagnalls New Standard Dictionary (1946 edition) | Oxford English Dictionary and its Supplements | Official Scrabble Players Dictionary | Random House Dictionary | Webster's New Collegiate Dictionary (Eighth edition) | Webster's New International Dictionary (Second edition) | Webster's Third New International Dictionary |
|---|---|---|---|---|---|---|---|---|---|---|---|
| ud | | | | | | ✓ | | | | | |
| ug | ✓ | ✓ | | | ✓ | ✓ | | | | ✓ | |
| uh | | | | | | ✓ | | | | | |
| um | | ✓ | | ✓ | | ✓ | | | | ✓ | ✓ |
| un | ✓ | ✓ | ✓ | | | ✓ | ✓ | ✓ | | ✓ | ✓ |
| up | ✓ | ✓ | ✓ | ✓ | ✓ | ✓ | ✓ | ✓ | ✓ | ✓ | ✓ |
| ur | ✓ | ✓ | | | ✓ | ✓ | | | | ✓ | ✓ |
| us | ✓ | ✓ | ✓ | ✓ | ✓ | ✓ | ✓ | ✓ | ✓ | ✓ | ✓ |
| ut | ✓ | ✓ | ✓ | | ✓ | ✓ | ✓ | ✓ | ✓ | ✓ | ✓ |
| uz | | | | | | ✓ | | | | | |
| va | | | | | ✓ | ✓ | | | | ✓ | |
| vd | | | | | | | | | | | ✓ |
| ve | | | | | | O | | | | | ✓ |
| vi | | | | | | | | | | | ✓ |
| vo | | | | | | ✓ | | | | | |
| vs | | | | | | | | ✓ | ✓ | ✓ | ✓ |
| vy | | | | | | O | | | | | |
| wa | | | | | | ✓ | | | | ✓ | ✓ |

| | Chambers Twentieth Century Dictionary (1972 edition) | Chambers Twentieth Century Dictionary (1983 edition) | Collins English Dictionary | Concise Oxford Dictionary (1982 edition) | Funk and Wagnalls New Standard Dictionary (1946 edition) | Oxford English Dictionary and its Supplements | Official Scrabble Players Dictionary | Random House Dictionary | Webster's New Collegiate Dictionary (Eighth edition) | Webster's New International Dictionary (Second edition) | Webster's Third New International Dictionary |
|---|---|---|---|---|---|---|---|---|---|---|---|
| we | ✓ | ✓ | ✓ | ✓ | ✓ | ✓ | ✓ | ✓ | ✓ | ✓ | ✓ |
| wi | | | | | | O | | | | | |
| wo | ✓ | ✓ | ✓ | ✓ | ✓ | ✓ | ✓ | ✓ | | ✓ | ✓ |
| wp | | | | | | O | | | | | |
| wr | | | | | | O | | | | | |
| ws | | | | | | | | ✓ | ✓ | ✓ | ✓ |
| wu | | | | | | O | | | | | ✓ |
| wy | | | | | ✓ | ✓ | | | | ✓ | ✓ |
| xa | | | | | | O | | | | O | |
| xi | ✓ | ✓ | ✓ | ✓ | ✓ | | ✓ | ✓ | ✓ | ✓ | ✓ |
| xs | | | | | | | | ✓ | ✓ | ✓ | ✓ |
| xu | | | | | | | ✓ | | ✓ | | |
| ya | | | | | ✓ | ✓ | ✓ | ✓ | | ✓ | ✓ |
| yd | | | | | | O | | | | | |
| ye | ✓ | ✓ | ✓ | ✓ | ✓ | ✓ | ✓ | ✓ | ✓ | ✓ | ✓ |
| yf | | | | | | O | | | | | |
| yi | | | | | | ✓ | | ✓ | | | |
| yk | | | | | | O | | | | | |

| | Chambers Twentieth Century Dictionary (1972 edition) | Chambers Twentieth Century Dictionary (1983 edition) | Collins English Dictionary | Concise Oxford Dictionary (1982 edition) | Funk and Wagnalls New Standard Dictionary (1946 edition) | Oxford English Dictionary and its Supplements | Official Scrabble Players Dictionary | Random House Dictionary | Webster's New Collegiate Dictionary (Eighth edition) | Webster's New International Dictionary (Second edition) | Webster's Third New International Dictionary |
|---|---|---|---|---|---|---|---|---|---|---|---|
| yl | | | | | | O | | | | | |
| ym | | | | | | O | | | | ✓ | |
| yn | | | | | | O | | | | ✓ | |
| yo | ✓ | ✓ | | | ✓ | ✓ | | ✓ | | ✓ | ✓ |
| yr | | | | | | ✓ | | | | ✓ | |
| ys | | | | | ✓ | ✓ | | ✓ | ✓ | ✓ | ✓ |
| yt | | | | | O | ✓ | | | | ✓ | |
| yu | ✓ | ✓ | | | ✓ | O | | | | ✓ | |
| yw | | | | | | O | | | | | |
| za | | | | | O | | | ✓ | | ✓ | |
| ze | | | | | | ✓ | | | | | |
| zo | ✓ | ✓ | ✓ | | | ✓ | | | | ✓ | |
| zs | | | | | | | | ✓ | ✓ | ✓ | ✓ |
| zy | | | | | | ✓ | | | | | |
| Total = 230 | 95 | 101 | 76 | 71 | 115 | 189 | 87 | 111 | 94 | 177 | 144 |

However, in a game of Scrabble, you might choose to disallow certain classes of words, even though they appear in the dictionary. For example, you might decide to exclude:

— obsolete words, even though there is nothing in the rules of the game which bars their use
— reformed spellings if they are given in your dictionary
— the names of all letters (such as AITCH, EPSILON and WYE) and their plural forms (such as BS, KAPPAS and ARS)
— those words which 'look' like abbreviations (such as BB, TV and VD), even though the dictionary may not refer to them as such
— those words from *Webster's Third New International Dictionary* which are marked 'often cap.' and 'usu cap.'. (*Webster's Third* lists almost every proper name with a lower-case letter, and then adds a label to indicate whether the word is capitalized, usually capitalized, often capitalized, or sometimes capitalized – all of which can be a bit frustrating for the Scrabble player.)

Of the 230 words given in the charts here, only 53 of them, less than a quarter, appear in all 11 of the dictionaries used. These 53 words can be taken as the hard core of two-letter words. They are: AD, AH, AI, AM, AN, AS, AT, AX, AY, BE, BY, DO, EH, EL, EM, EN, EX, FA, GO, HA, HE, HI, ID, IF, IN, IS, IT, JO, LA, LI, LO, MA, ME, MI, MU, MY, NO, OF, OH, ON, OR, OX, PA, PI, RE, SI, SO, TI, TO, UP, US, WE and YE.

No attempt has been made to define the 230 words in the lists here. The main reason for this is that the same word may be defined quite differently in different dictionaries. For example, OE is defined by *Webster's Third New International Dictionary* as a violent whirlwind off the Faroe Islands; the 1983 *Chambers* dictionary defines OE as a grandchild; and yet *The Random House Dictionary* gives both of these definitions, plus a third one: a nephew or niece. A second example: the 1983 *Chambers* dictionary offers two definitions of DA; a heavy Burmese knife, and a dialect form of 'dad'. *Webster's Third* has the second of these, but not the first, and it also defines DA as a valuable fibre plant! To add to the confusion, *The Official Scrabble Players Dictionary* defines DA as a preposition meaning 'of' or 'from'. It seems that not only do dictionaries differ tremendously in which two-letter words they do or do not list, they also provide a startling variation in the associated definitions!

Just to dismay the Scrabble player even further, these 230 two-letter words are not the ultimate collection. By going to other dictionaries, progressively more specialized, additional two-letter specimens can be unearthed. The following are just a few examples. IG is an obsolete form of the personal pronoun, I, and can be found in *Webster's New International Dictionary* (First Edition); IX is another name for the axle-tree, and appears in *A Dictionary of Archaic and Provincial Words*, by James Orchard Halliwell-Phillipps; OZ is a ration of narcotics, and is given in *Dictionary of American Slang*, by Wentworth and Flexner; and UI is an isthmus, and is listed in Joseph Wright's *The English Dialect Dictionary*. Of course, none of these is a source that the Scrabble player would expect to use, but they do demonstrate the wealth of two-letter words which can be tracked down.

# *THE OFFICIAL SCRABBLE PLAYERS DICTIONARY*

*The Official Scrabble Players Dictionary* (*OSPD*) has been mentioned several times. The *OSPD* is the official dictionary of first reference for all Scrabble tournaments throughout the United States and Canada. It was prepared by Selchow and Righter, the US manufacturers of Scrabble. The *OSPD* does not have any official status in Great Britain, but will frequently be referred to in *The Scrabble Omnibus* as this book is published widely outside Great Britain.

# 4

# INSIDE THE SCRABBLE PLAYER'S MIND

What goes through a Scrabble player's mind before he or she makes a particular move during a game of Scrabble? Merely watching a Scrabble player's moves will tell you little of the thought processes behind them, particularly if you are trying to learn to improve your game. How does an expert player decide which letters to play and which to keep? How does he decide when to change poor letters and when to play them? How does he decide it may be better to play a certain word for 70 points than to play some other word for 85 points? How does an expert decide when to chance playing a word that he is not sure of?

Here are three fully annotated games. Six expert players made brief notes of their thoughts during each of the games. Their notes have been expanded, and their thoughts are encapsulated in the comments here.

The experts don't necessarily always make the best moves at each turn. Occasionally they miss the best moves, or see them when it's almost too late. And sometimes they make bad mistakes. You might be able to improve on the experts' moves in the three games here. You might disagree with some of their reasoning. Nevertheless, you should find their comments instructive. In all three games, blank tiles are represented by asterisks.

# ANNOTATED GAME NUMBER 1

*The 1983 edition of* Chambers Twentieth Century Dictionary *was used. The 'house rules' for this particular game allowed the use of obsolete words and letter names, as long as they appear in the dictionary.*

## PLAYER A

ADLRRUU
I don't like two Rs and two Us. I must get rid of RU and something else. I decide to play LUR for 6 points, and hang on to ADRU.

ADEIRSU
I know this set of letters! It makes just one word, RESIDUA, the plural of RESIDUUM.

## PLAYER B

EEFIJR+
I can't see a 7-letter word here, nor an 8-letter using anything on the board. Should I play EF, keeping EIJR+ to try for a bonus with a J in it? Or should I play the J somewhere? I decide not to be greedy, and opt for JEE and LURE, leaving me with FIR+. That scores 30 points.

AEEFIR+
I can see FAERIES on my rack, and LEAFIER. But I can't see how to get either of them down

48

## PLAYER A

Should I play RESIDUA and LA, or RESIDUA and AJEE? Or perhaps use the L of LURE for RESIDUAL? I go for the second of these, RESIDUA and AJEE. That gets 77 points.

### EIMOORV

Do I play MOVE, leaving IOR? Or how about MOVIE, using the I of RAREFIE*? I spot VROOM, using the R of RAREFIE*, and since this will leave me with EIR, I go for it, even though it scores slightly fewer points than MOVIE. VROOM scores 26.

### EINRSTZ

No word here. I know that EINRST can be combined with 18 other letters, but Z isn't one of them. I'll hang on to the EINRST and just play the Z. There's a convenient triple-letter-score square just above the second O of VROOM. ZO fits in nicely, and I'm pleased with the 31 points it scores.

### AEINRST

Magic! The best seven letters I could hope for. Lots of options here. I've got the usual batch of anagrams that can be made from these letters (such as NASTIER, RETAINS and STAINER). LURES and STAINER would get 69 points. The U of LURE could be used to make URANITES or URINATES, both for 77 points. Better still, the P of POSED would give PAINTERS or PANTRIES for 83 points. And the M of MALIC would give MINARETS, also

## PLAYER B

on the board. I wonder about using the R, E, L or U already on the board. The U doesn't look promising; the E and the R are letters I already have; so I concentrate on the L. I toy with FLEA+IER, but can't think what the blank ought to be. I give up on that. I go back to the two Rs on the board, in LURE and RESIDUA. Either of those will give me RAREFIE+ to get the blank as a D or an S. I use the R of RESIDUA as the second R of RAREFIE* to get the double-word score. That's 72 points. I nominate the blank as an S.

### CEMOPSS

COMPOSES straight out of the bag! What luck! But will it go down? I consider CLURE as a possibility, but reject it. Is there a spare R for COMPOSERS? No! I decide to break up the letters, and I go for POSED and VROOMS. I don't like using the S and leaving myself with three consonants, but I've got to make a score. I take the 38 points, and hope I don't decide later that this was a bad move.

### ACLMNOS

The C and the M left from the last turn aren't doing me much good. I really ought to ditch them. I consider using the I of RAREFIE*, and making a word that takes in the nearby triple-word-score square. I spot MALIC for 27 points, leaving myself with NOS. That's not too bad.

### EINNOST

I see INTONES straightaway. Usual problem, though – I can't get it down anywhere. What about LONNIEST, PONNIEST, RONNIEST, SONNIEST or TONNIEST? None sounds at all likely. Then I recall the word TONTINES, using the T of MINARETS. I take it thankfully for 70 points.

## PLAYER A

for 83 points. I choose MINARETS in preference to PAINTERS and PANTRIES, but for no real reason.

### BEGLOOW
BELOW? ELBOW? BLOW? GLOW?
Et cetera. Why not use the L to turn RESIDUA into RESIDUAL, coming down with a four- or five-letter word ending in L? BOWEL is about the best, and gets me 38 points.

### DGIOPTU
Nothing special here. What about a six-letter word ending in D, making DZO at the same time? I can't see one. Or how about a five-letter word beginning with the B of BOWEL? BIGOT is worth 27 points, and leaves me with DPU. Not great, but I do get to keep the U, and the Q is still to come. I play BIGOT for 27 points.

### ADILPQU
I've picked the Q! It's just as well I held on to the U. QUAIL, QUAD, QUID, QUIP – these are all possibles. I can't see a six-letter word ending in D, to make DZO in the top left-hand corner. I could use the I of TONTINES to make QADI for 28 points. I didn't need to hold on to the U after all. I finally go for SUQ, using the blank S of RAREFIE*. 31 points. Not bad!

## PLAYER B

### AACFINT
This doesn't look very hopeful. I think about playing the ACF somewhere, then I spot the seven-letter FANATIC. Almost missed it! I can almost play it parallel to TONTINES, making IF, NA, EN and SA, but SA isn't in *Chambers*. I can't see anywhere else to put FANATIC. Why am I plagued with seven-letter words that won't go down! I decide to use the C or F, or both if possible, and to cover the triple-word-score square beneath the S of TONTINES. CAST would score 27; FAST would get 30. Better still, I spot FISC for 39 points. I'm not keen on being left with two As, but I can live with it. I take the 39 points.

### AAIKNRT
KAT for 14 points? OAK for 14? Or KAE for 17? They'll all leave me with ANRT. I choose KAE, adding 17 points to my score.

### AGINORT
I see ORATING. And I suspect ROATING is okay, too. Again, neither will fit in at all. What about GROATING, using the G of BIGOT? Or CROATING? Or ACTORING? No, these don't seem likely. Using the T of BIGOT, I wonder about TROATING. It sounds vaguely familiar, but I can't put a meaning to it. I'll chance it anyway – it's worth a risk for the 80 points. My opponent does challenge TROATING, but it's acceptable. TROAT is a verb meaning 'to bellow'. I don't think I shall forget that one!

## PLAYER A

### ADILOPT

TOPLAID? POTLAID? POTDIAL? These all run through my mind and are instantly dismissed. Completely irrelevantly, I recall a placename DIAL POST, a small village in Sussex, England. How about that six-letter word ending in D in the top left-hand corner? Is it in sight yet? I think about POTLID. Is it in the dictionary? If it is, it might be hyphenated, or even two words. I won't chance it. What about IDOL, OD, WO and EL for 21 points, leaving me with AIPT? Or ADOPT, LURED and EA for 24 points, leaving me with IL? No, I go for PO, PO and OW for a marginally-better 25 points. And I've still got the D!

### ADEHILT

Is there a six-letter word ending in D, I ask myself again. Yes, I spot HAILED, which is worth 46 points. HALTED is worth 46 too. I wonder about LATHED. That would be worth 55 points. But I'm not sure about LATHE as a verb. To turn on a lathe or similar device? Sounds risky! I go for HAILED and DZO for 46 points.

### AINTXY[+]

An interesting collection of letters. My first thought is to get rid of the X and Y somewhere, holding on to AINT[+]. Then I spot ANXIETY, using the blank as an E. Incredible! But will it go down anywhere at this advanced stage of the game? I wonder about FEVERY. I know FEVERISH, and I think FEVEROUS exists, but I just don't know about FEVERY. If I play ANXIETY and FEVERY, my opponent is bound to challenge FEVERY. I would! If it's not in the dictionary, I'll have blown it. I'm 31 points behind. Can I catch up without risking FEVERY? I could play AX, AX and HA in the top left-hand corner for 41 points; or even better, XI, XI and IN, parallel to TROATING, for 52 points. Either of those moves would

## PLAYER B

### ABEHRVY

Four high-scoring letters here. Perhaps I should change. Let's see what else I can do before rushing into a change. HERBY? HEAVY? HAVE? HAVER? BRAVE? Could VERBY exist? That seems unlikely. Using the T of TONTINES, I could play BATH for 26 points. I could put down EH, EH and OWE for 26, too. Or I could play HI, HA and AN, next to TROATING, for 28. Or HI, HE and EN in the same place for the same score. I'd like to get rid of at least two of the high-scoring letters, so I go for BATH, leaving me with ERVY. That's not great. Maybe I should have changed. Still, I take the 26 points.

### EEGRUVY

FEVER, using the F of FISC, would leave me with GUY. Does FEVERY exist, or is there just FEVERISH? I can't see much else, so I play FEVER for 22 points.

### DDGNUWY

So, my opponent has the X. He's got several places to go, so I ought to block the best of them, next to TROATING. But what with? My own letters are pretty uninspiring. Besides just blocking my opponent, I've got to go for a reasonable score, otherwise he'll still be able to overtake me. GU, GI and UN is worth 16 points; and DUG, DA, UT and GI is better still, 21 points. I take the 21 points, wondering whether this will be sufficient to stop my opponent from galloping past me.

## PLAYER A

leave me with the blank. I now spot another seven-letter word, TAXYING, using the blank as a G. Will this go down anywhere? I've still got to risk FEVERY to get this down. But at least it would score better than ANXIETY as it stretches across a double-word-score square. How likely is it my opponent will go out? There are eight letters left, DDGNTUWY, and he's got seven of them. With rubbish like that, he won't be going out quickly. So if I do chance FEVERY, and it isn't there, he won't be able to go out, and then I'll have another chance of playing my X. Reluctantly, I play TAXYING and FEVERY. Both are challenged by my opponent. TAXYING is okay; but not FEVERY. No points!

### AINTXY[+]
Terrible move, that last one! I don't know why I didn't go for XI, XI and IN, instead of being greedy and coming unstuck. Now even that place has gone. With a sigh, I play AX, AX and HA in the top left-hand corner for 41 points.

### INTY[+]
I'm 40 points behind, and my opponent's got DTW, 7 points. If I go out and catch him, I need 26 points to draw, or 27 to win. I don't think I can do it. Using the blank as an S, I could play FEVERS and STY for 21 points. Not good enough! I opt for YIN, YE and EN, for 23 points, still leaving me with IT[+].

### IT[+]
My opponent's got DT, and I'm still behind, by 28 points. I need 22 to draw, or 23 to win. I could play LIST and SUQS for 15 points, or FEVERS and SIT for 15 points, neither of which is good enough. I ponder for a while, see nothing better, and reluctantly play FEVERS and SIT, and take my last 15 points. My opponent is caught for 3 points, which I add on to my score and deduct from his, but

## PLAYER B

### DNTWY
All the letters have gone now, and my opponent still has a blank. Can I keep ahead? WIN, WE and EN gets 23 points, leaving me with DTY, and ANY, IN and NY gets 29 points, leaving DTW. I take the 29 points.

### DTW
My opponent's still 17 points behind. He might still be able to manage something with his blank, but I can't see what. And I can't go out in one move with DTW. I play AW and OWE for 11, leaving DT.

52

## PLAYER A

he's still won, by just 7 points! It's all my own fault for risking FEVERY when I could have played safe. I'm sure I would have won if I'd avoided FEVERY. Ah well!

## PLAYER B

| H | A | I | L | E | D |  | P |  |  | B | I | G | O | T |
|---|---|---|---|---|---|---|---|---|---|---|---|---|---|---|
| A | X |  |  | Z | O |  | P | O |  |  |  | 2W |  | R |
|  |  | V | R | O | O | M | S | 2L | O | W |  | 2W |  | O |
| 2L |  |  | A | W |  |  | E |  |  | E | 2W |  | D | A |
|  |  |  | R | E | S | I | D | U | A | L |  |  | U | T |
|  | K | A | E |  | 3L |  |  | J |  |  |  |  | G | I |
|  | 2L | F |  |  | 2L |  |  | 2L |  | E | 2L |  |  | N |
| M | A | L | I | C |  | L | U | R | E |  | 2L |  |  | G |
| I | N | E |  |  | 2L |  |  | 2L |  |  | 2L |  |  | 2L |
| N | Y |  | + | U | Q |  |  | 3L |  |  |  | 3L |  |  |
| A |  |  | 2W |  |  |  |  | 2W |  |  |  |  |  |  |
| R |  | B |  |  | F | E | V | E | R | + |  |  |  | 2L |
| E | 2W | A |  | Y | I | N |  |  |  | I |  |  |  |  |
| T | O | N | T | I | N | E | S |  | 3L |  | T | 2W |  |  |
| S |  | H |  |  | C |  |  | 2L |  |  |  |  |  | 3W |

## THE WORDS AND SCORES SUMMARIZED

| PLAYER A | | | PLAYER B | | |
|---|---|---|---|---|---|
| Words | Scores | Running Totals | Words | Scores | Running Totals |
| LUR | 6 | 6 | JEE, LURE | 30 | 30 |
| RESIDUA, AJEE | 77 | 83 | RAREFIES (S = blank) | 72 | 102 |
| VROOM | 26 | 109 | POSED, VROOMS | 38 | 140 |
| ZO | 31 | 140 | MALIC | 27 | 167 |
| MINARETS | 83 | 223 | TONTINES | 70 | 237 |
| BOWEL, RESIDUAL | 38 | 261 | FISC | 39 | 276 |
| BIGOT | 27 | 288 | KAE | 17 | 293 |
| SUQ | 31 | 319 | TROATING | 80 | 373 |
| PO, PO, OW | 25 | 344 | BATH | 26 | 399 |
| HAILED, DZO | 46 | 390 | FEVER | 22 | 421 |
| challenged | 0 | 390 | DUG, DA, UT, GI | 21 | 442 |
| AX, AX, HA | 41 | 431 | ANY, IN, NY | 29 | 471 |
| YIN, YE, EN | 23 | 454 | AW, OWE | 11 | 482 |
| FEVERS, SIT (S = blank) | 15 | 469 | | | |
| | +3 | 472 | | −3 | 479 |

# ANNOTATED GAME NUMBER 2

*The 1983 edition of* Chambers Twentieth Century Dictionary *was used. The 'house rules' for this particular game did not allow the use of obsolete words or letter names. This is in line with the rules used at the British National Scrabble Championship.*

## PLAYER A

AEIKNNP
Should I play PINK, leaving AEN, or INK, leaving AENP? Can I make a five-letter word beginning or ending with K? KNAP I know, but not KNAPE or KNIPE. I choose INK, because I can hook on to it later, perhaps with my P. I take INK's 14 points.

## PLAYER B

ABHHIVY
Dreadful letters. Perhaps I should change straight off. I could play HAY and INKY, leaving BHIV. That's worth 28 points. And then there's YAH and KY for 26 points. I decide to play HAY and INKY. I hope I don't regret not changing BHHVY.

54

## PLAYER A

**AENOPQT**

I decide to change the Q. I want to keep a balanced rack with the same number of vowels and consonants. I also throw back the OP with the Q, hanging on to just AENT. No points here.

**AENOTWX**

I can't play XI, XI and IN, above INKY, because the house rules of this game bar letter names, whether from the English alphabet or the Greek alphabet. XI's no good to me here. I see WAX, HOW and AHA for 36 points, and WAX and WINKY for 44 points. I'm not sure about WINKY, so I'm not prepared to risk it for the extra 8 points. I'm also conscious of the fact that though WINKY sounds familiar, it may be because of the nursery rhyme character Wee Willie Winkie. I take the 36-pointer.

**EINNORT**

With VENTILS, my opponent has created the possibility of a nine-timer, a word covering the two triple-word-score squares on the top row. But the V doesn't make it easy. I think of INTERVON, a non-existent word. How about NONRIVET? I guess not! I give up on the nine-timer, and return to my own seven letters by themselves. I've got INTONER and TERNION on my rack. There's INTONER and RINKY – but I'm not at all sure of the latter. I settle for TERNION and IN, well aware that I'm opening up the chance for another nine-timer in the far left column. It's worth the 62 points, though.

**ADELSZ+**

Good letters, the blank, an S and the Z. I see DAZZLES right away. DAZZLES and SIN is worth 81 points, but I'd like more than that for using an S, a Z and a blank. Can I get a double-double using the I of TERNION, perhaps ending in -IZE, -IZED or -IZES? How

## PLAYER B

**BHINOSV**

Still dreadful letters! Should I change this time? I like the idea of playing BOH, HO and AH, leaving me with INSV. I don't usually like being left with a V, but V does go quite nicely with INS. I choose this, settling for 26 points.

**EILNSTV**

EILNST is a potent group of letters. It combines with well over half the letters of the alphabet to make a valid seven-letter word. I know that the only word possible from these seven letters is VENTILS. I spot VENTILS and IS for 65 points, and VENTILS and SI also for 65 points. Much better, though, is VENTILS, HOWL and AHAS for 90 points. I play that.

**ADEGIRY**

Two nine-timers are possible now, but with these letters, I don't have much of a chance. I could use the T of TERNION, and play GYRATED for 36 points. Or I could use the V of VENTILS to play GRAVID. I choose GRAVID, thinking that by holding on to the Y, I might be able to pick up a healthy 20–30 points next time. GRAVID scores 36 points.

**AAEFQRY**

I ought to change AFQY, but let's see what I can score anyway. I see FAERY on my rack, but can't see anywhere too useful to put it on the board. I see FA, IF and ZOA for 26 points, and also FY and WAXY for one point less. I play FY and WAXY. I've ditched two

## PLAYER A

about DUALIZES? I know DUALISM and DUALIST, but I don't think that either DUALISE or DUALIZE exist. I know ODAL, but what about ODALIZES? Doesn't sound at all likely. I wonder about DIALIZES? No, that second I ought to be a Y. Hang on! Using the I of TERNION, and using the blank as a Y, I could make DIALYZES. That's worth 84 points. Finally, I decide to just play the Z, making ZO and ZINKY. I am half hoping that with a good pick-up I might be able to get the nine-timer across the T of TERNION.

ADELSS+

Two Ss and a blank! I've got SADDLES and SLASHED, neither of which will go down anywhere. I'm drawn to the T of TERNION. Is there a word beginning ST, and probably ending with an S? Various possibilities occur: STADDLES, STADILES, STALIDES, STARDLES and STRADLES. I dismiss STADILES; I'm sure I'm influenced here by the word STABILE. STALIDES sounds like chemicals, but STAL- is a meaningless prefix or combining form in chemistry. STARDLES is suggested by STARTLES, I'm sure. And STRADLES must be suggested by STRADDLES. That just leaves STADDLES. It sounds vaguely familiar, but I can't imagine what it means. I wonder about STANDLES or STANDELS – I recall an American pop group of some years ago called the Standells! Concentrate! I think I'll chance STADDLES. If it's there, I'll score 140 points, and if it's not there, I can almost certainly get my bonus at the next turn. I play STADDLES, using the blank as the first D. My opponent challenges it, but it's okay – thank goodness! Apparently, a STADDLE is a support for a haystack. That rings absolutely no bells at all with me.

CEJMOOP

COME, COPE, MOPE, POEM, POME, JO, JOE and even the odd-looking JOCO all come

## PLAYER B

awkward letters, and so stand twice the chance of picking up a U to go with my Q.

AAEQRVW

Definitely time for a change! I put back AQVW, and hang on to AER. No points.

ABEENPR

AMBER or EMBER for 30 points, using M of COMPO? Or BE, EM and BO for 28? I settle

56

## PLAYER A

to mind. What about ZOOM for 17 points? JIN, JO and ON is no good. There's JINN, but not JIN. I could play JOE, GO and RE for 19 points; or ZOO, OO and IO for 20; or even COMPO and GO for 24 points. I take the 20, and leave myself with EJ.

### AAEIJMR
JEE for 26, using the second E of AMPERE? Or RAJA and FA for 32? I like the second one, because it scores better, leaves me with EIM, a not unreasonable collection, and it does start to open the bottom part of the board. I take 32 points.

### EIIMNRT
I can see INTERIM and MINTIER immediately. But will they go down? I expect not. I also spot TERMINI, which is probably an acceptable plural form of TERMINUS. That won't go anywhere either. I shall have to make an opening. I use the T of VENTILS and just play a solitary I, making the word TI. Even if my opponent takes it, I've still got letters in TERNION and ROBING to think about for a possible eight-letter word. TI scores a pathetic 2 points.

### EEIMNRT
As I expected, my opponent took the opening presented by TI. Ah well! Is there TERMINE,

## PLAYER B

on AMPERE for 33 points. That leaves me with BN. Let's hope I pick up some vowels.

### ABGINOS
Is there a spare T for BOASTING? No, of course not! Isn't GABIONS a word? I'm sure I've seen it before, something to do with forts. Playing it parallel to RAJA would make FAN, JO and AI – all okay – and RB, which doesn't exist, of course. Can I do anything with the spare R of TERNION? BORGAINS? BAGNOIRS? Or BOARINGS? No, I don't think any of these are words. But BAGNOIRS reminds me of BAGNIO, a noun, I think. Isn't it a brothel? Can I play the plural form, BAGNIOS, anywhere? No, it's as hopeless as GABIONS! Could the plural be BAGNIOES, with the ES ending? I could play that across the E of TERNION, also making SO and AS. But I don't see BAGNIOES as the correct plural form. I give up! What about playing ROBING, using the R of RAJA? That scores 36, and leaves me with AS. I take it.

### AEELSTU
I recognize this group of letters. There's ELUATES and the doubtful SETUALE. I think the latter might be obsolete, and obsolete words aren't allowed in this game. Anyway, I thank my opponent for his TI, and I play ELUATES and TIE for a very acceptable 78 points.

### EEIOQUU
I changed the Q earlier and it has come back. At least I've got a U to go with it this time. I

## PLAYER A

perhaps a short form of DETERMINE or TERMINATE? I don't think so. If there was, I could play it parallel to ELUATES, making TE and ES in the process. How about TERMINER, using the R in TERNION. I seem to recall a legal phrase 'oyer and terminer'. I don't know what it means, but I'm sufficiently confident to try TERMINER for 72 points. My opponent challenges it, but only half-heartedly. He seems to think it will be okay. We check the dictionary, which indicates that it is a legal term. The dictionary just defines it as 'the act of determining'.

### CEGLORW

CROW and WO, using the O of OUZO, is worth 23 points. COLE, TO, EL and RE scores 26. WORE, TO, ER and RE is worth 30. And FAW and WOG scores 32. I make the last of these moves, leaving myself with CELR.

### ACDELOR

There's hardly any room left on the board for a bonus, not that I've got a chance of one with these letters. I briefly consider CORDABLE, using the B of ROBING, and CAROLED. But the latter would have two Ls, surely? More realistically, I consider the bottom right-hand corner. Is there a five-letter word that I can fit in there? RACED, LACED and ARCED will all fit, but ACRED is better because the C is on a double-letter-score square. That's a useful 34 points.

### LO

I see ten points for LO, LI and ON, using the IN of TERMINER. One point better is LOO, LA

## PLAYER B

could make QUEUE across the E of TERMINER for 14 points; or QUEUE across the first E of AMPERE for 14 points. Neither is inspiring. I decide to play OUZO for 15 points, hoping that I will pick up some letters which will allow me to get a reasonable score with the Q. We shall see!

### EEIQTU[+]

This is more like it! I've picked up a blank and a T. I see QUIETED, QUIETEN and QUIETER, but can't see where they'll go. QUIETER also anagrams to REQUITE, but that doesn't do me any good either. What about an eight-letter word? I concentrate on the BING of ROBING. The N is the most likely of these four. I quickly see QUEENITE, using the blank as yet another E! I think a QUEENITE is a queen's supporter or some such. I play it for 70 points, but it's a shame I haven't managed to double the Q or the word as a whole.

### DFITUV

That's all the letters gone. My six are horrible, and my opponent is 43 points ahead. I can't see me winning this game. My opponent only has two letters left, LO if I've counted right, and is bound to go out on the next turn. I need to get rid of as many letters as I can, concentrating on shifting the F and V. Using the E of ACRED, I can play FIVE for 20 points, leaving me with DTU. Or I can play FUD, OF and GU for 27, leaving me with ITV. I see nothing better, so I take the 27.

58

# PLAYER A

and OP for 11 points. I take the 11. I've caught my opponent with ITV, so add 6 points to my score, and deduct 6 points from his. A reasonable win!

# PLAYER B

| 1 | 2 | 3 | 4 | 5 | 6 | 7 | 8 | 9 | 10 | 11 | 12 | 13 | 14 |
|---|---|---|---|---|---|---|---|---|----|----|----|----|----|
| 3W |  |  | 2L |  | L | A |  | G | R | A | V | I | D |
|  | 2W | T |  | C | O | M | P | O |  |  | E | 2W |  |
|  |  | E |  | O | P | 2L |  |  |  |  | N |  |  |
| 2L |  | R | 2W |  | E |  |  |  | 2W |  | T | I | E |
|  |  | M |  | 2W |  |  |  | B |  |  | I |  | L |
|  | 3L | I |  | O | E |  |  | H | O | W | L | 3L | U |
|  |  | N |  | U | 2L |  | 2L | A | H | A | S |  | A |
| S |  | E | 2L | Z | I | N | K | Y |  | X |  |  | T |
| T | E | R | N | I | O | N |  | 2L |  | F | Y | 2L | E |
| A | 3L |  |  | 3L |  | R | A | J | A |  |  | 3L | S |
| + |  |  | 2W |  |  | O |  |  | W | O | G |  |  |
| D |  | 2W |  |  |  | B |  |  |  | F | U | D | 2L |
| L |  | 2W |  |  | 2L | I | 2L |  |  |  | 2W |  |  |
| E | 2W | Q | U | E | E | N | I | T | + |  |  | 2W |  |
| S |  | 2L |  |  |  | G |  |  | A | C | R | E | D |

## THE WORDS AND SCORES SUMMARIZED

| PLAYER A | | | PLAYER B | | |
|---|---|---|---|---|---|
| Words | Scores | Running Totals | Words | Scores | Running Totals |
| INK | 14 | 14 | HAY, INKY | 28 | 28 |
| change | 0 | 14 | BOH, HO, AH | 26 | 54 |
| WAX, HOW, AHA | 36 | 50 | VENTILS, HOWL, AHAS | 90 | 144 |
| TERNION, IN | 62 | 112 | GRAVID | 36 | 180 |
| ZINKY, ZO | 32 | 144 | FY, WAXY | 25 | 205 |
| STADDLES (first D = blank) | 140 | 284 | change | 0 | 205 |
| COMPO, GO | 24 | 308 | AMPERE | 33 | 238 |
| RAJA, FA | 32 | 340 | ROBING | 36 | 274 |
| TI | 2 | 342 | ELUATES, TIE | 78 | 352 |
| TERMINER | 72 | 414 | OUZO | 15 | 367 |
| FAW, WOG | 32 | 446 | QUEENITE (third E = blank) | 70 | 437 |
| ACRED, EA | 34 | 480 | FUD, OF, GU | 27 | 464 |
| LOO, LA, OP | 11 | 491 | | | |
| | +6 | 497 | | −6 | 458 |

# ANNOTATED GAME NUMBER 3

*This was played under the same rules as the second annotated game, using the 1983 edition of* Chambers *as the dictionary of authority, with obsolete words and letter names being barred.*

## PLAYER A

ADELMRS

It's a shame I have to start. If my opponent had gone first and played a word with an E in it, which is quite likely, then I could go out with EMERALDS. But he hasn't, so I can't. I know the adjective DERMAL, but I'm sure it can't be used as a noun, so DERMALS is no good. I go for LAM for 10 points. I can always turn it into SLAM, LAME or LAMS if I need to.

## PLAYER B

AABINKV

Dreadful letters! I see BINK and AVA and AVIAN and BANK and KAVA. Should I play any of these or should I change? I'm about to play VIA and LAMA, leaving me with ABKN, when I decide to play those letters instead and keep AIV. I could play BANK and LAMA, with the K falling on a triple-letter-score square. I also know the word NABK, a kind of bush or shrub. I'll play that instead of BANK. It's a

## PLAYER A

**DEENORS**

I knew NABK and had no intention of challenging it. With my letters, I've got ENDORSE. Is there an anagram of it? I don't think so. Anyway, it doesn't matter. ENDORSE will do just fine, pluralizing NABK, and going across two double-word-score squares. ENDORSE and NABKS scores 93. I'm off to a good start!

**ADEHPRS**

SHARPED springs to mind. I'm sure that SHARP is a verb, meaning the same as SHARPEN. I could play SHARPED and ENDORSED for 74 points, SHARPED and ENDORSEE for 87, or SHARPED and ENDORSER for 87. And SHARPED and DAD is worth 87 too. Of course, PHRASED is an anagram of SHARPED! I almost missed it. That's much better, because PHRASED and ENDORSES is worth 93 points. Two 93s together is certainly something. I take the 93 points.

**ADIJNOR**

A loose E would give me ADJOINER, and there was a loose E, in ENDORSE, until VILAYET was played. I'm not totally sure about ADJOINER, anyway. Perhaps it's just as well I've been stopped from playing it. There's JAB, TAJ and MA for 28 points; and ADJOIN and DAN for 35 points. Best of all is HADJ, for 45 points.

**IMNOORW**

I need to ditch at least WO, and maybe even MOW. I decide on WO, WE and ON for 16 points. IMNOR is what I'm left with.

## PLAYER B

more interesting word! LAMA and NABK get me 26 points, leaving me with AIV.

**AEEIVXY**

I see ENDORSEE and VEX, or YEX, both for 35 points. I'd prefer to play VEX and keep the Y than the other way round. The quicker I get rid of my Vs, the better. Slightly better is AX, OX and DA, parallel to ENDORSE. That's worth 37 points. I could play one of my Es, making AXE, OX, DA and RE for 40 points. This leaves me with EIVY. I take the 40 points, feeling that perhaps I should have played the V. Let's see how it turns out.

**EILTVY$^+$**

LEVITY plus a blank. What can I do with this little lot? The V and Y together don't look inspiring. VIOLETY? I think not. EVICTLY, VENTILY, VESTILY and EVILITY all cross my mind, but I reject the lot of them. But VILAYET is a word, I do know that. It's a province or region, I recall. I can't do VILAYET and DAT, because DAT isn't in the dictionary. I see VILAYET, EL and TA for 69 points. I take it, pleased to get the V and Y out. I didn't think it was going to be possible.

**CFGINRY**

Another bad group of letters. Using OX already on the board, I see COXING and FOXING for 48 and 51 points respectively. I play FOXING. That's not as bad as I thought it might be. I'm now left with CRY, which isn't great, but it could be worse.

**CEEINRY**

I need to get rid of CEY, leaving me with the balanced rack of EINR. I spot ICY and WEY for 25 points. That'll leave me with EENR, which is almost as good as EINR. I take the 25 points.

## PLAYER A

### GIMNOOR

I've got MOORING and ROOMING here. I could play MOORING and RICY for 83 points. How about ROOMING and MICY for 85 points? But surely the word is MOUSY, not MICY? Then I realise that the G of FOXING can be used to make GROOMING. If the G already on the board is used as the final G of GROOMING, I'll score 89. But if it's used as the initial G of GROOMING, then the M falls on the double-letter-score square, and that scores 95 points. Two 93s and now a 95! Where will it end?

### AEERTVW

I need to get rid of the V and W, and I've probably got to use one of the two Es to do it. I play WIVE, DAW and REV for 39 points, leaving me with the excellent AERT.

### AEOQRTU

I've got EQUATOR, but it won't go down anywhere. A loose Z (some hopes!) would give me QUATORZE. I decide to play the Q. QUAG is my best bet for 24 points.

### CEINORT

I can see RECTION from these letters. Using the S of SLIGHTED, I can play RECTIONS for 83 points. Not bad. But the position of the S on the top row invites a nine-timer. Can it be done, I wonder. I look for an eight-letter word ending in -ISE or -IST or -EST or -IEST. I conjure with CONTRISE, ONCERIST, RECONIST and NECROIST, but all are useless. Then I see CORNIEST. Beautiful! It scores a massive 149 points. I can't believe my luck!

## PLAYER B

### EEILNRS

I know that RELINES is allowed, and LIERNES, too. I spot SENILER, but I don't like these strained comparatives. I'd rather avoid SENILER if I can, though I'd quite happily play it if there was nothing else. I have to play LIERNES and RICY. The R of LIERNES is in just the right place. That's 77 points. My opponent challenges LIERNES. We check the dictionary, and find it's okay. A LIERNE is a cross-rib in vaulting, whatever that means!

### AEHLOPR

Turning RICY into PRICY and taking the triple-word-score square in the bottom left-hand corner could be quite profitable. Let's see what can be done. PARE, PRICY, AN, RE and ES is worth 52 points. So is PORE in the same position. Better still is OPERA, OE, PRICY, EN, RE and AS. That gets 57 points. I take it.

### EGHILST

SLEIGHT is an obvious word here, though it won't fit in – as usual! But the D of HADJ enables me to play SLIGHTED for 80 points. I'll settle for that.

### AIOTUZ[+]

Words like ZO, ZOA, ZATI, AUTO, TUI and TUZA come to mind. I'm sure TUZA isn't in *Chambers*, though. It was in another dictionary which I regularly played by some years ago. I'll have to forget it for this game. I wonder about AUTOLIZE. I know of a process called 'autolysis'. But perhaps the verb is AUTOLYSE or AUTOLYZE. Either way, it's not worth pursuing. I could get 35 points for OOZY, using the Y of VILAYET, but I'd need to use my blank. I could get 38 for TOZE, TA, OY, ZEL and ETA, again by using my blank as the E. I decide to keep the blank, and just play

## PLAYER A

ABDEITU
A spare T somewhere would give me
DUBITATE. No such luck, though. My ABE
plus the L of VILAYET suggest an -ABLE
ending. I fiddle around with DITU, and finally
see DUTIABLE. I'm sure that'll be okay. I play
it for 78 points. My opponent challenges it,
we check it, and it turns out to mean exactly
what I thought it ought to mean: subject to
customs duty.

U
What can I score with my solitary U? With the
T of OUTFIT, I can have UT for two points.
The G of SLIGHTED gives me UG for three
points, or GU for four points. But I decide to
play BUR for five points, using the B of
NABKS and the R of PHRASED. I'm out and
my opponent is caught with T$^+$. I add one
point to my score, and deduct a point from
his. The final scores are 648 to me and 473 to
my opponent. That's pretty good scoring! I
had five bonuses, three of them in the 90s and
one of them a nine-timer. I'm pleased.

## PLAYER B

the Z for whatever it'll get. I see ZOA and
NAP for 29 points. That'll do nicely.

FIOTTU$^+$
OUTFITS is on my rack, but it won't go on the
board at this late stage of the game. Using the
T of DUTIABLE gives me OUTFITT$^+$, just one
letter short of OUTFITTER. Using the A of
DUTIABLE, I wonder about FUTATION. I
know REFUTATION, but I can't see
FUTATION existing by itself. I pass it over.
Since my opponent has just one tile left, I've
got to use as many of my tiles as I can. I settle
for OUTFIT, scoring a measly 20 points. I'm
left with T$^+$.

## THE WORDS AND SCORES SUMMARIZED
### PLAYER A

| Words | Scores | Running Totals |
|---|---|---|
| LAM | 10 | 10 |
| ENDORSE, NABKS | 93 | 103 |
| PHRASED, ENDORSES | 93 | 196 |
| HADJ | 45 | 241 |
| WO, WE, ON | 16 | 257 |
| GROOMING | 95 | 352 |
| WIVE, DAW, REV | 39 | 391 |

### PLAYER B

| Words | Scores | Running Totals |
|---|---|---|
| NABK, LAMA | 26 | 26 |
| AXE, DA, OX, RE | 40 | 66 |
| VILAYET, EL, TA (A = blank) | 69 | 135 |
| FOXING | 51 | 186 |
| ICY, WEY | 25 | 211 |
| LIERNES, RICY | 77 | 288 |
| OPERA, OE, PRICY, EN, RE, AS | 57 | 345 |

| | | | | | | |
|---|---|---|---|---|---|---|
| QUAG | 24 | 415 | SLIGHTED | 80 | 425 |
| CORNIEST | 149 | 564 | ZOA, NAP | 29 | 454 |
| DUTIABLE | 78 | 642 | OUTFIT | 20 | 474 |
| BUR | 5 | 647 | | | |
| | +1 | 648 | | −1 | 473 |

```
3W  .   .   D   .   .   .   C   O   R   N   I   E   S   T
.   2W  .   U   .   3L  .   .   .   3L  .   .   .   L   .
.   O   U   T   F   I   .   T   .   2L  .   .   .   2W  I
2L  .   .   I   .   .   .   2L  .   .   .   2W  .   G   2L
.   .   .   A   2W  .   .   .   .   .   Z   .   .   H   .
.   3L  .   B   .   3L  .   .   .   3L  O   .   .   T   .
.   V   I   L   +   Y   E   T   2L  N   A   P   2L  E   .
3W  .   .   E   .   .   L   A   M   A   .   H   A   D   J
.   L   2L  .   .   .   2L  .   2L  B   U   R   2L  .   .
.   I   .   .   W   O   .   F   .   K   .   A   .   3L  .
O   E   .   .   E   N   D   O   R   S   E   S   .   .   .
P   R   I   C   Y   .   A   X   E   .   .   E   .   .   Q
E   N   2W  .   .   .   W   I   V   E   .   D   2W  .   U
R   E   .   .   .   3L  .   N   .   3L  .   .   .   2W  A
A   S   .   2L  .   .   .   G   R   O   O   M   I   N   G
```

# 5

# SCRABBLE PUZZLES

There are 25 puzzles here. Each puzzle shows the board at a certain stage in a game and the seven tiles that one player has at that stage. For each of the puzzles, you must try to make the highest score possible with the seven tiles on the board shown. Of course, in a full game, the best move might not necessarily be the one with the highest score. In real games, it is often wise to take a slightly lower score than the best possible in order to leave yourself with better letters for your next move, or to make things slightly more difficult for your opponent. In the puzzles here, blank tiles are represented by crosses.

All of the words in these puzzles and in their best solutions appear in both *Chambers Twentieth Century Dictionary* (1983 edition) and *The Official Scrabble Players Dictionary*, with a few exceptions. The exceptions are words of nine or more letters, which are not listed in *The Official Scrabble Players Dictionary*.

## SCRABBLE PUZZLE 1

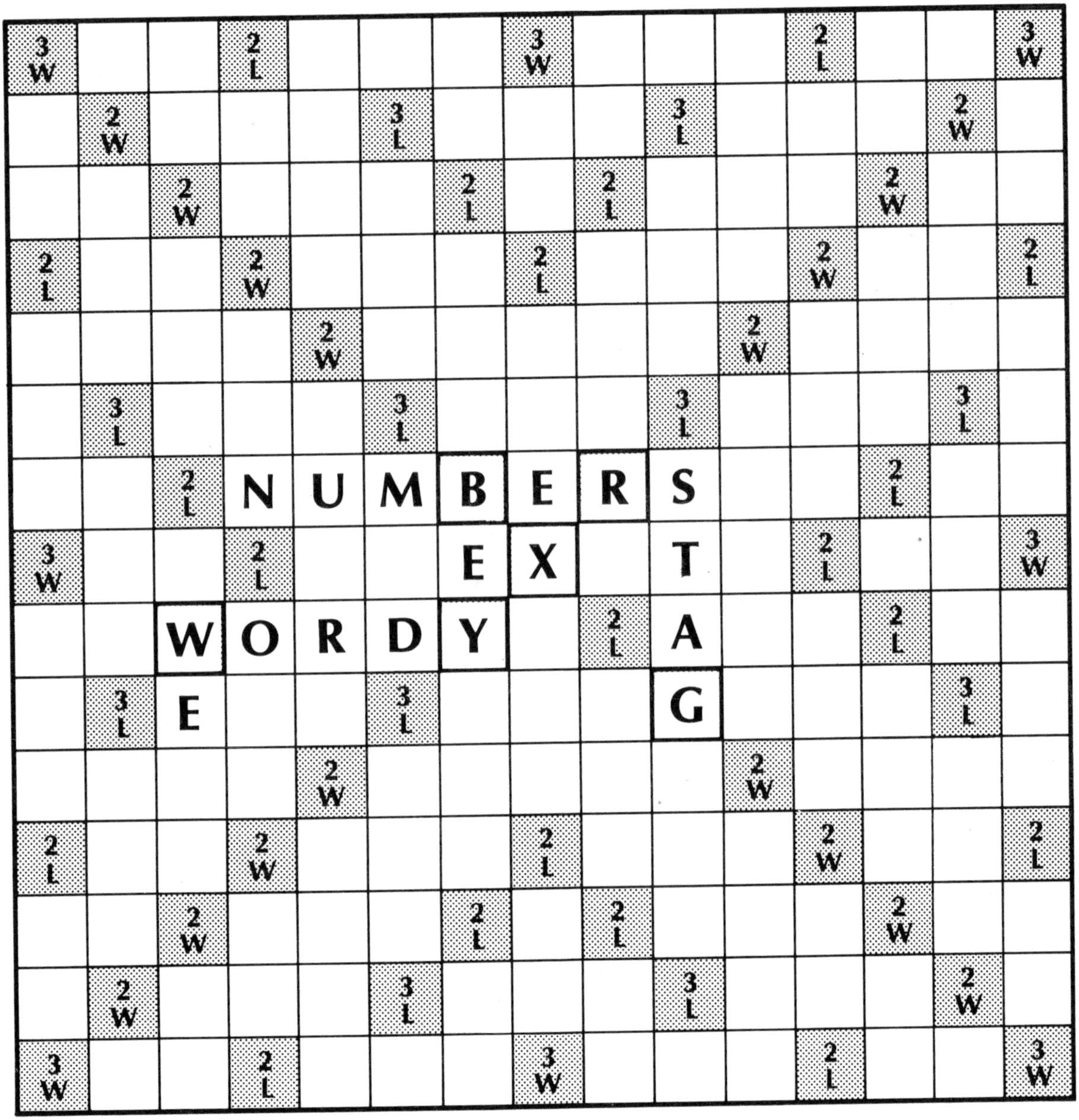

**D  E  L  N  O  R  U**

# SCRABBLE PUZZLE 2

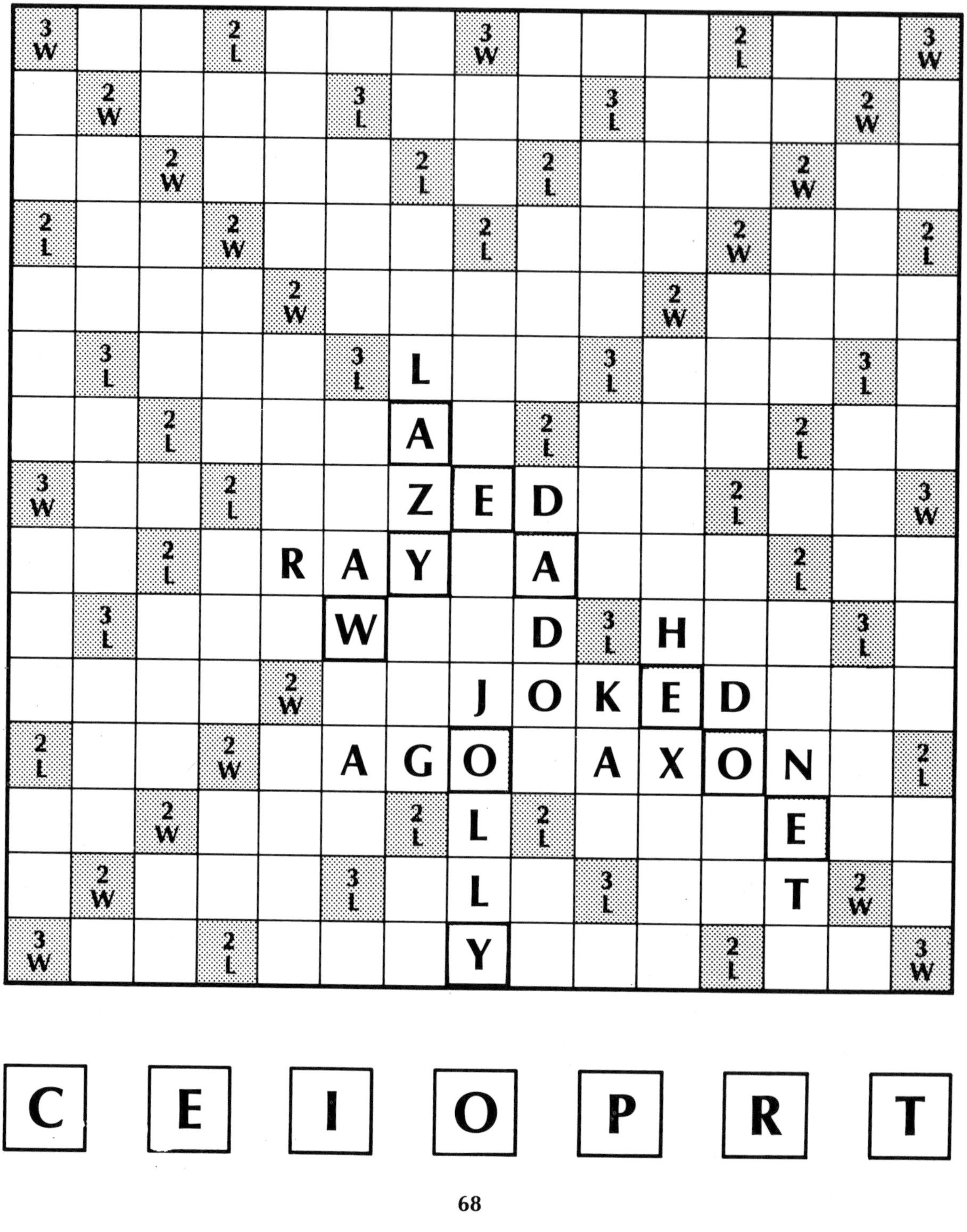

A 15×15 Scrabble board with the following letters placed:

- Row 6: **L**
- Row 7: **A**
- Row 8: **Z** **E** **D**
- Row 9: **R** **A** **Y** **A**
- Row 10: **W** **D** **H**
- Row 11: **J** **O** **K** **E** **D**
- Row 12: **A** **G** **O** **A** **X** **O** **N**
- Row 13: **L** **E**
- Row 14: **L** **T**
- Row 15: **Y**

Available letters: **C** **E** **I** **O** **P** **R** **T**

# SCRABBLE PUZZLE 3

69

# SCRABBLE PUZZLE 4

| | | | | | V | | | | | | | Q | | |
|---|---|---|---|---|---|---|---|---|---|---|---|---|---|---|
| | | | | | O | | | | | | | U | | |
| | | | | | L | | | | | | | I | | |
| | M | E | N | T | A | L | | | | | | N | O | D |
| | E | | | | R | E | | | | | | I | | |
| | W | | | | | A | | | B | A | R | N | | |
| | | | | | | P | | | E | | | E | | |
| | N | O | V | E | L | I | S | T | A | | | | | |
| | | | | | | | O | | R | O | B | | | |
| | | | | | | | R | | | | I | | | |
| | | | | | | | C | A | N | T | O | | | |
| | | | | M | Y | T | H | | | | N | | | |
| | | W | E | E | | | | | | | I | | | |
| | A | | | | | | | | | | C | H | E | Z |
| | X | | | | | | | | | | S | | | |

| A | E | O | R | T | U | + |
|---|---|---|---|---|---|---|

# SCRABBLE PUZZLE 5

The grid contains the following letters (with Scrabble premium-square markings such as 3W, 2W, 3L, 2L):

```
[3W] U  P  [2L]        I  [3W] S  C  A  N  T        [3W]
     [2W] E      [3L] G     A  [3L]              [2W]
 E       R          L  A  Y              [2W]
 R  E  M  I  T       O  [2L]          [2W]          P
              E  G  O           [2W]                U
 M  [3L]       E  [3L]              [3L]       G  [3L] N
 E  R  R  A  N  D  S        [2L]          F  I  A  T
[3W]       W        O  V  A           I  T        [3W]
 Z  O  N  E        Y     D  U  K  E  [2L]
 O  X           [3L]       D  [3L]          [3L]
 O           [2W]          L        [2W]             C
 N        [2W]       B  R  E  D        [2W]          A
       [2W] J  I  V  E     [2L] I     B  A  I  L
    [2W] E     O           S     U        [2W]     L
[3W] A  I  T     W  [3W] T  H  I  N           [3W]
```

Tray letters:

**E  F  H  O  R  S  +**

71

# SCRABBLE PUZZLE 6

| | | | | | | | | | | | | | | |
|---|---|---|---|---|---|---|---|---|---|---|---|---|---|---|
| 3W | | | 2L | | | | 3W | | | | 2L | | | 3W |
| | 2W | | | L | 3L | E | | | 3L | | | | 2W | |
| | | 2W | | A | | V | | 2L | | | | 2W | | |
| 2L | | V | I | M | | E | 2L | | | | 2W | | | 2L |
| | | | F | E | R | R | O | U | S | 2W | | | | |
| | 3L | | | | 3L | | | | P | | | | 3L | |
| | | 2L | | | | 2L | | 2L | E | | | 2L | | |
| 3W | | | 2L | | | | C | H | A | T | E | A | U | 3W |
| | | 2L | | M | | 2L | O | 2L | R | | | 2L | | |
| | 3L | E | R | O | T | I | C | | 3L | | J | | 3L | |
| | | | | B | O | | K | A | Z | O | O | | | |
| 2L | | | 2W | | T | | Y | | E | | Y | E | N | 2L |
| | | 2W | | | A | 2L | | 2L | D | | I | 2W | | |
| | 2W | H | A | L | L | O | W | S | 3L | | N | | 2W | |
| 3W | | A | W | | | | 3W | | | | G | | | 3W |

B F L O S U X

# SCRABBLE PUZZLE 7

73

# SCRABBLE PUZZLE 8

# SCRABBLE PUZZLE 9

# SCRABBLE PUZZLE 10

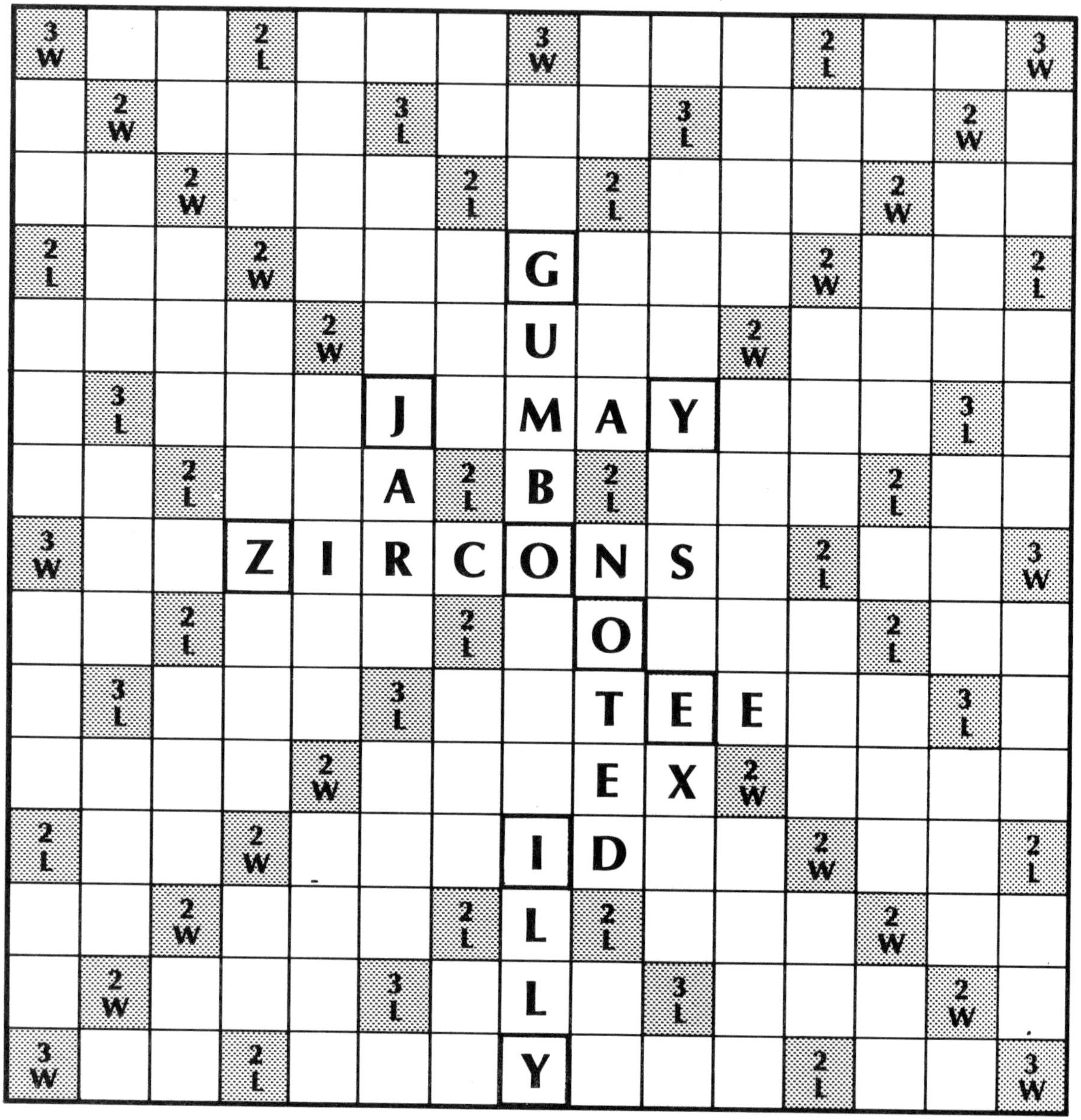
G
U
J M A Y
A B
Z I R C O N S
O
T E E
E X
I D
L
L
Y

A I N Q S T +

# SCRABBLE PUZZLE 11

| | | | | | | | | | | | | | | |
|---|---|---|---|---|---|---|---|---|---|---|---|---|---|---|
| 3W | | | 2L | | | | 3W | | Z | E | B | R | A | 3W |
| E | 2W | | | | 3L | | P | | O | | | | 2W | |
| X | | 2W | | | | 2L | A | G | O | | | 2W | | |
| T | | | 2W | F | | | 2L | O | | | 2W | | | 2L |
| A | M | I | D | E | | | | L | | 2W | | | | |
| N | 3L | | | N | O | T | E | D | 3L | | | | 3L | |
| T | | 2L | | | | 2L | V | 2L | | | | 2L | | |
| 3W | | | 2L | | | | E | G | G | H | E | A | D | 3W |
| | | 2L | | | O | W | N | 2L | | I | | 2L | | |
| J | O | T | T | E | R | | | | 3L | T | | | 3L | Q |
| U | | | | 2W | E | L | F | | | C | O | Y | P | U |
| M | | | 2W | | | | I | | | H | E | | | A |
| B | | 2W | | | | 2L | V | 2L | | | | 2W | | C |
| O | 2W | | | | 3L | | E | | 3L | | | | 2W | K |
| 3W | | | 2L | | | | 3W | | | | 2L | | | 3W |

| | | | | | | |
|---|---|---|---|---|---|---|
| I | I | S | S | S | S | + |

# SCRABBLE PUZZLE 12

| | | | | | E | M | I | T | T | I | N | G | | |
|---|---|---|---|---|---|---|---|---|---|---|---|---|---|---|
| | | | | | | | | | R | | | | | |
| | | | | P | | | | I | | | | | | |
| U | | | O | H | O | | J | O | G | | | | | |
| R | A | N | D | | R | | | | G | E | | E | | |
| I | | | | | T | A | B | L | E | | C | | | |
| N | | | | | | A | | R | | U | | | | |
| A | | | | | W | A | V | E | D | | | | | |
| T | | | | | R | | | D | O | | | | | |
| E | T | E | N | S | I | O | N | | F | | | | | |
| | | | | | T | | | | F | | | | | |
| | | | | | E | | | | S | K | I | | | |
| | | | | | R | | | | | | | | | |
| | | | | | S | | | | | | | | | |
| | | | | | | | | | | | | | | |

## E H L O P X +

# SCRABBLE PUZZLE 13

|   |   |   |   |   |   |   |   |   |   |   |   |   |   |   |
|---|---|---|---|---|---|---|---|---|---|---|---|---|---|---|
| 3W |  |  | 2L |  |  |  | 3W |  |  |  | 2L |  |  | 3W |
|  | 2W |  |  |  | 3L |  |  |  | 3L |  |  |  | 2W |  |
|  |  | 2W |  |  | A | 2L |  | 2L | I | L | L |  | 2W |  |
| 2L |  |  | 2W |  | T | O | T | A | L | L |  | 2W |  | 2L |
|  |  | O |  | 2W |  | D |  |  | L | L | 2W |  |  |  |
| 3L |  | E | X |  | 3L | D |  |  | 3L |  |  | I |  | 3L |
|  | 2L | E |  |  |  | E |  | 2L |  |  |  | R |  |  |
| 3W |  | N | I | T | R | A | T | E |  | S | A | G |  | 3W |
|  | 2L |  |  |  | E | 2L |  | 2L | C |  | T |  |  |  |
|  | 3L | A | Y |  | R |  | Q | U | I | R | E | 3L |  |  |
|  |  | E | O | N |  |  | U |  | 2W | O |  | O |  |  |
| 2L |  | A |  |  |  | 2L | I |  |  | O | T | I | C |  |
|  |  | 2W |  | A | M | A | Z | E |  | M | 2W | L |  |  |
|  | 2W |  |  | 3L |  |  | 3L |  |  |  | Y |  |  |  |
| 3W |  | 2L |  |  |  | 3W |  |  |  | 2L |  |  | 3W |  |

**A   D   E   H   K   O   V**

# SCRABBLE PUZZLE 14

| | | | | | | | | | | | | | | |
|---|---|---|---|---|---|---|---|---|---|---|---|---|---|---|
| 3W | | | 2L | | | | 3W | | | | 2L | | | 3W |
| | 2W | | | | 3L | | | | 3L | | | | 2W | |
| | | 2W | | | | 2L | | 2L | | | | 2W | | |
| 2L | | | 2W | | | | 2L | | | | 2W | | | 2L |
| | | | | 2W | | | | | | O | R | E | | |
| | 3L | | | | 3L | | | | 3L | | I | | 3L | |
| | | 2L | | Z | | 2L | | 2L | R | | N | 2L | | |
| 3W | | | T | O | | | C | L | U | C | K | | | 3W |
| | | 2L | H | O | | 2L | I | 2L | M | | | 2L | | |
| | 3L | | U | | 3L | | V | | 3L | | | | 3L | |
| | | E | M | 2W | | | V | E | X | E | D | | | |
| 2L | | | B | E | N | D | Y | | | | O | A | T | 2L |
| | | 2W | I | | | 2L | | 2L | | | | 2W | I | |
| | 2W | | N | | 3L | | | | 3L | | | W | E | |
| 3W | | | G | | | | 3W | | | | 2L | | | 3W |

| | | | | | | |
|---|---|---|---|---|---|---|
| A | D | H | I | J | O | Y |

# SCRABBLE PUZZLE 15

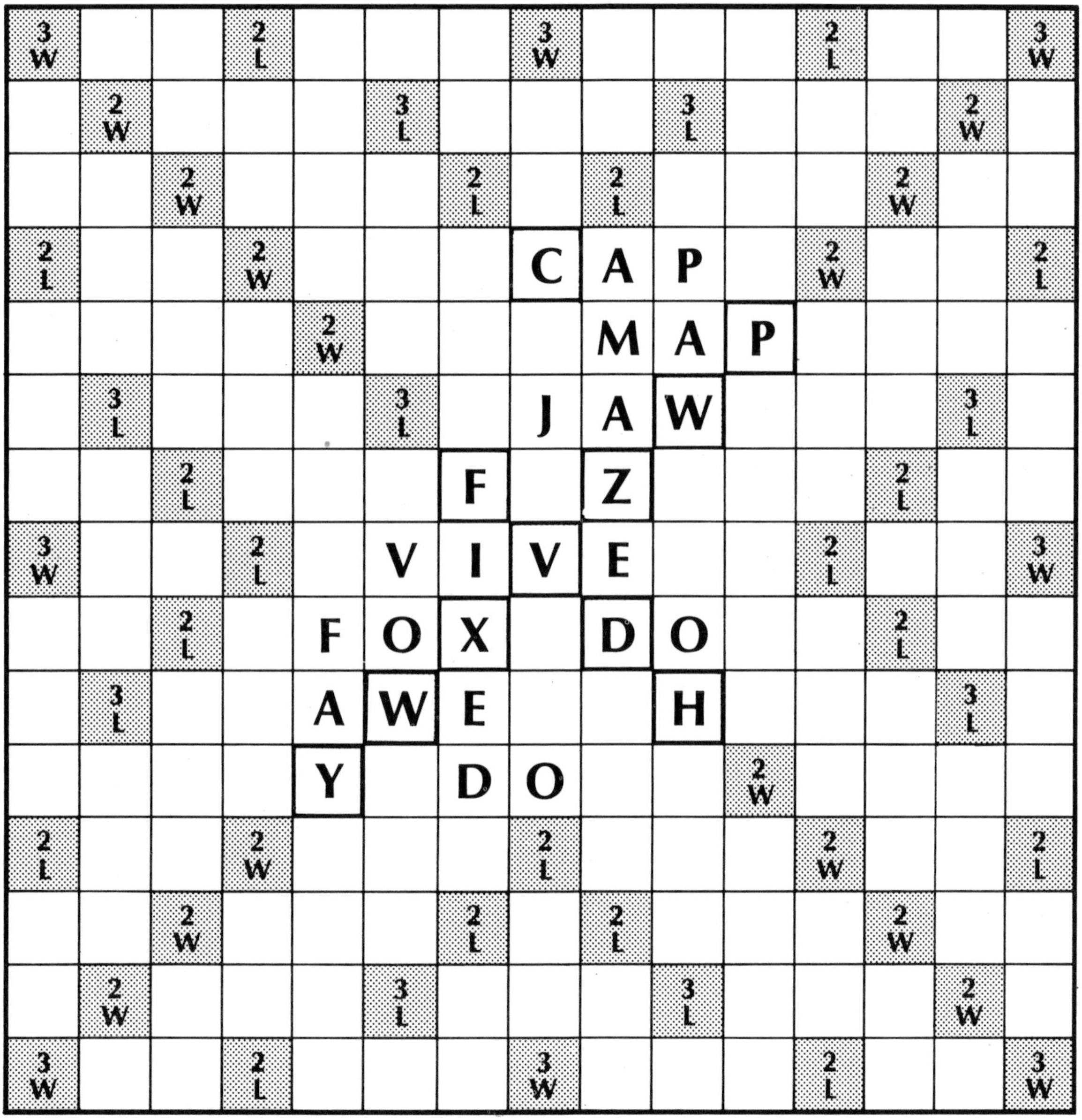
CAP
MAP
JAW
F Z
VIVE
FOX DO
AWE H
Y DO

A E I I O R U

# SCRABBLE PUZZLE 16

| B | D | K | O | R | W | Y |
|---|---|---|---|---|---|---|

# SCRABBLE PUZZLE 17

A D E I I O U

# SCRABBLE PUZZLE 18

A E E G R S T

84

# SCRABBLE PUZZLE 19

| | | | | | | | | | | | | | | |
|---|---|---|---|---|---|---|---|---|---|---|---|---|---|---|
| 3W | | | 2L | | | | 3W | | | | 2L | | | 3W |
| | 2W | O | | | 3L | | | | 3L | | | | 2W | |
| | A | W | N | | | 2L | | 2L | | | | 2W | | |
| 2L | | | A | | | | 2L | | | | 2W | | | 2L |
| | | | M | 2W | | | | | | 2W | T | H | E | |
| | 3L | | E | | 3L | | | | 3L | | O | | 3L | |
| | | 2L | D | O | | 2L | | 2L | | F | A | 2L | | |
| 3W | | | 2L | Y | | | W | I | V | E | D | | | 3W |
| | | 2L | | E | V | E | R | 2L | | L | | 2L | | |
| | 3L | F | E | Z | 3L | | I | | 3L | L | | | 3L | |
| | | E | | 2W | | | T | | | 2W | | | | |
| 2L | E | L | L | | D | I | E | T | E | R | S | | | 2L |
| | | T | I | | | 2L | | 2L | | | P | 2W | | |
| | 2W | | D | | 3L | | | | 3L | | A | | 2W | |
| 3W | | | 2L | | | | 3W | | | | 2L | | | 3W |

B E G N O R Y

# SCRABBLE PUZZLE 20

|   |   |   |   |   |   |   |   |   |   |   |   |   |   |   |
|---|---|---|---|---|---|---|---|---|---|---|---|---|---|---|
| 3W |   |   | 2L |   |   | E | 3W |   | T |   | 2L |   |   | 3W |
|   | 2W | P | E | R | I | L |   |   | H |   |   |   | 2W |   |
|   |   | A |   |   | K | A | Z | O | O |   |   | 2W |   |   |
| 2L |   | W | 2W |   |   | 2L |   |   | R |   | 2W |   |   | 2L |
| A | C | E | D |   | 2W |   |   |   | A | 2W |   |   |   |   |
|   | 3L | D |   |   | 3L |   |   |   | X |   |   |   | 3L |   |
|   | 2L |   |   |   | 2L |   | 2L | E | V | A | D | E |   |   |
| 3W |   | H | A | R | P | I | E | S |   | 2L |   |   | 3W |   |
|   | 2L |   |   |   | 2L | N |   |   |   | 2L |   |   |   |   |
|   | 3L |   |   | 3L |   | T | 3L |   |   |   | 3L |   |   |   |
|   |   | 2W |   |   | A |   | 2W |   |   |   |   |   |   |   |
| 2L |   | 2W |   |   | 2L | I |   | 2W |   |   | 2L |   |   |   |
|   | 2W |   |   | 2L | E | L |   |   | 2W |   |   |   |   |   |
|   | 2W |   | 3L |   | R |   | 3L |   |   |   | 2W |   |   |   |
| 3W |   | 2L |   |   | A |   |   |   | 2L |   |   | 3W |   |   |

**A  B  D  E  N  V  W**

86

# SCRABBLE PUZZLE 21

| | | | | | | | | | | | | | | |
|---|---|---|---|---|---|---|---|---|---|---|---|---|---|---|
| 3W | | | 2L | | | | 3W | | | | 2L | | | 3W |
| | 2W | | | | 3L | | | M | A | N | I | A | 2W | |
| | | 2W | | | | 2L | | I | | | | 2W | | |
| 2L | S | E | D | I | T | I | O | N | | | 2W | | | 2L |
| | | | O | 2W | | | | A | | 2W | | | | |
| | 3L | E | X | | 3L | O | A | R | 3L | | | | 3L | |
| | | 2L | Y | | | 2L | | E | | | | 2L | | |
| 3W | | | 2L | | | | A | T | | | 2L | | | 3W |
| | | 2L | | | | 2L | P | 2L | | | | 2L | | |
| | 3L | | | | 3L | | P | | 3L | R | A | N | 3L | |
| | | | | 2W | | | L | O | B | E | | | | |
| 2L | | | 2W | A | I | R | Y | | A | | 2W | | | 2L |
| | | 2W | | | | 2L | | 2L | R | | | 2W | | |
| | 2W | | | | 3L | | | | 3L | | | | 2W | |
| 3W | | | 2L | | | | 3W | | | | 2L | | | 3W |

A C E H K R T

# SCRABBLE PUZZLE 22

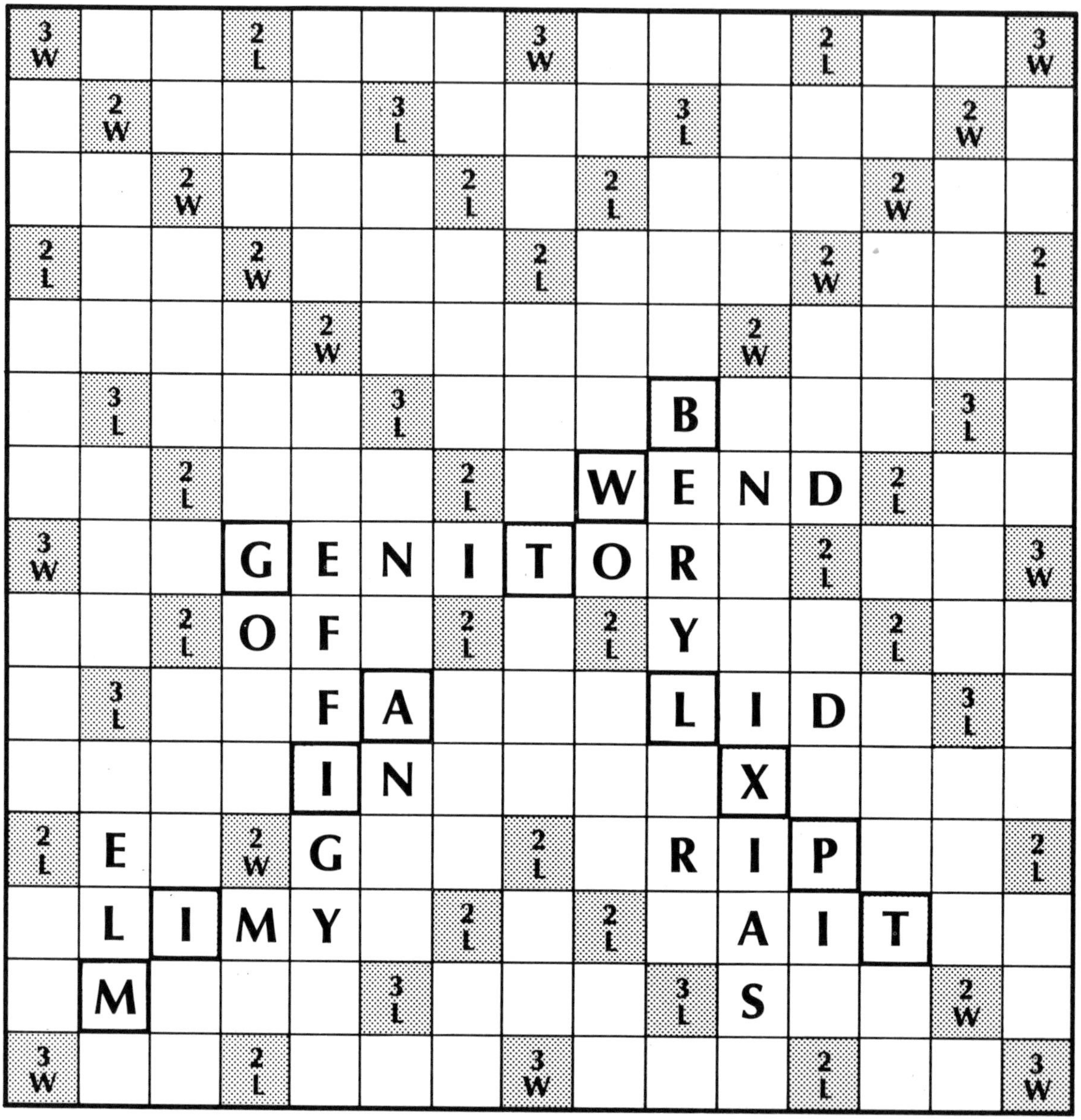
B
WEND
GENITOR
O F Y
FA LID
IN X
E G RIP
LIMY AIT
M S

A C D R S U +

# SCRABBLE PUZZLE 23

On the board are the words: EXHAUST, HARVEST, OIL, ROAD, AM.

Rack letters: **A D E N O R U**

# SCRABBLE PUZZLE 24

The grid contains the following words:

TARRING
OVEN
EARTH
MARS
LECTOR
REGNANT
SWAM

with the down words: TAVE (TEVIL?), VARO, RAT, RIO, GOIMARIA, etc.

Letter tiles available:

| C | E | H | L | P | P | S |
|---|---|---|---|---|---|---|

# SCRABBLE PUZZLE 25

| | | | | | | | | | | | | | | |
|---|---|---|---|---|---|---|---|---|---|---|---|---|---|---|
| 3W | | | 2L | | | | 3W | | | | 2L | | | 3W |
| | 2W | H | | | A | D | D | R | E | S | S | | 2W | |
| | | O | W | E | D | 2L | A | 2L | | | I | 2W | | |
| 2L | | V | 2W | | | | 2L | | | | 2W | | | 2L |
| | | E | | 2W | | | | O | | A | | | | |
| | O | R | | | 3L | S | T | R | I | P | P | E | D | |
| | V | 2L | | | T | 2L | | E | | E | E | L | | |
| 3W | A | M | B | I | E | N | T | | | | R | | | 3W |
| | | A | | | A | 2L | O | X | T | A | I | L | | |
| | 3L | | | | 3L | | | | E | | | I | 3L | |
| | | | A | 2W | | | | | N | 2W | | K | | |
| 2L | | | R | E | L | I | A | N | T | | F | I | N | 2L |
| | | 2W | C | | | 2L | J | 2L | | | | N | | |
| | 2W | | H | | C | L | E | W | 3L | | | G | 2W | |
| 3W | | | 2L | | | | E | | | | 2L | | | 3W |

G M R U Y Y +

# PUZZLES WITH A THEME

There are ten puzzles here. Each puzzle shows the board at a certain stage in a game, and the seven tiles that one player has on his rack at that stage. Each game has a theme, and you will see that all the words played in any one of these games are tied into the theme. For example, in the first puzzle here, the theme is 'animals'. All the words already on the board are animal names.

With the seven tiles given with each game, you must try to make the highest score possible on the corresponding board. All words you play must also tie in with the theme. In the puzzles here, blank tiles are represented by crosses.

All the words in these puzzles and their best solutions are in *Chambers Twentieth Century Dictionary* (1983 edition) and *The Official Scrabble Players Dictionary*. Not all the definitions are in *The Official Scrabble Players Dictionary*, since that dictionary usually gives only one definition against each word it lists. For example, the word QUAIL which appears on the board in the 'birds' puzzle is defined by *The Official Scrabble Players Dictionary* merely as a verb meaning 'to cower'. No reference is made to the bird called QUAIL. All the words and definitions are in *Webster's Third New International Dictionary*, as well as *Chambers Twentieth Century Dictionary*.

# 1. ANIMALS

All of the words on this board are animals. Plurals are allowed if you want to play them.

| | | | | | | | | | | | | | |
|---|---|---|---|---|---|---|---|---|---|---|---|---|---|
| Z | | | 2L | | | | W | | | 2L | | | 3W |
| E | 2W | W | | J | 3L | | O | | 3L | | | 2W | |
| R | O | E | | U | | 2L | L | 2L | | | A | 2W | |
| D | | A | M | O | U | F | F | + | O | N | | | 2L |
| A | | N | B | | | O | | 2W | O | | | | |
| | 3L | L | I | O | N | X | | 3L | | A | I | 3L | |
| | | I | | | 2L | | 2L | | | | N | | |
| 3W | | N | Y | L | G | H | A | U | | 2L | D | O | E |
| | | G | | E | | I | | 2L | | | R | | |
| | 3L | | M | I | N | K | | | 3L | | A | I | 3L |
| | | | U | | D | | D | E | E | R | | | |
| 2L | | | 2W | R | | | 2L | | | | G | | 2L |
| | | 2W | | | | 2L | | 2L | | | A | 2W | |
| | 2W | | | | 3L | | | | 3L | | L | | 2W |
| 3W | | | 2L | | | | 3W | | | | I | | 3W |

**A   A   B   C   P   R   Y**

93

## 2. BIRDS

The theme here is birds — singular, plural, flightless, extinct and any other kind are allowed.

Grid letters (Scrabble-style board):

- L, Q
- JABIRU
- JA, LINNET, QUAIL (A ... N ... A)
- CHIC+EN (CHICKEN), LINNET
- EN K A E LORY
- N D T
- A
- WAXWINGS
- MOA, SERIN
- O D, R, I, N
- DOVE
- ORR, RIN
- RH
- E
- N

Letter rack:

A  G  I  L  M  O  +

# 3. COLOURS

The theme here is colours, hues, shades, dyes, colouring matters and pigments.

| | | | | | | | | | | | | | |
|---|---|---|---|---|---|---|---|---|---|---|---|---|---|
| 3W | | | 2L | P | | S | A | N | G | U | I | N | E |
| | 2W | M | A | U | V | E | | 3L | R | | | 2W | |
| | | 2W | | R | 2L | | 2L | | E | | 2W | | |
| 2L | | 2W | | P | | | X | | E | 2W | | | 2L |
| | | | A | L | I | Z | A | R | I | N | | | 2L |
| | 3L | | | E | 3L | | N | V | | | | 3L | |
| | | 2L | | | 2L | T | | O | | | 2L | | |
| L | I | L | A | C | | C | H | E | R | R | Y | | 3W |
| U | | 2L | R | | 2L | I | 2L | Y | | | 2L | | |
| T | 3L | | E | B | O | N | | 3L | | | | 3L | |
| E | | | A | | | | | 2W | | | | | |
| O | | 2W | M | | | 2L | | | | 2W | | | 2L |
| L | A | K | E | | 2L | | 2L | | | | 2W | | |
| I | 2W | | | 3L | | | | 3L | | | | 2W | |
| N | | 2L | | | | 3W | | | | 2L | | | 3W |

| A | B | E | G | I | J | + |
|---|---|---|---|---|---|---|

95

## 4. DOGS

All words in this puzzle must be dogs, singular or plural. Of course, dogs don't necessarily have to be canine animals . . . There are HOTDOGS and all manner of non-canine dogs!

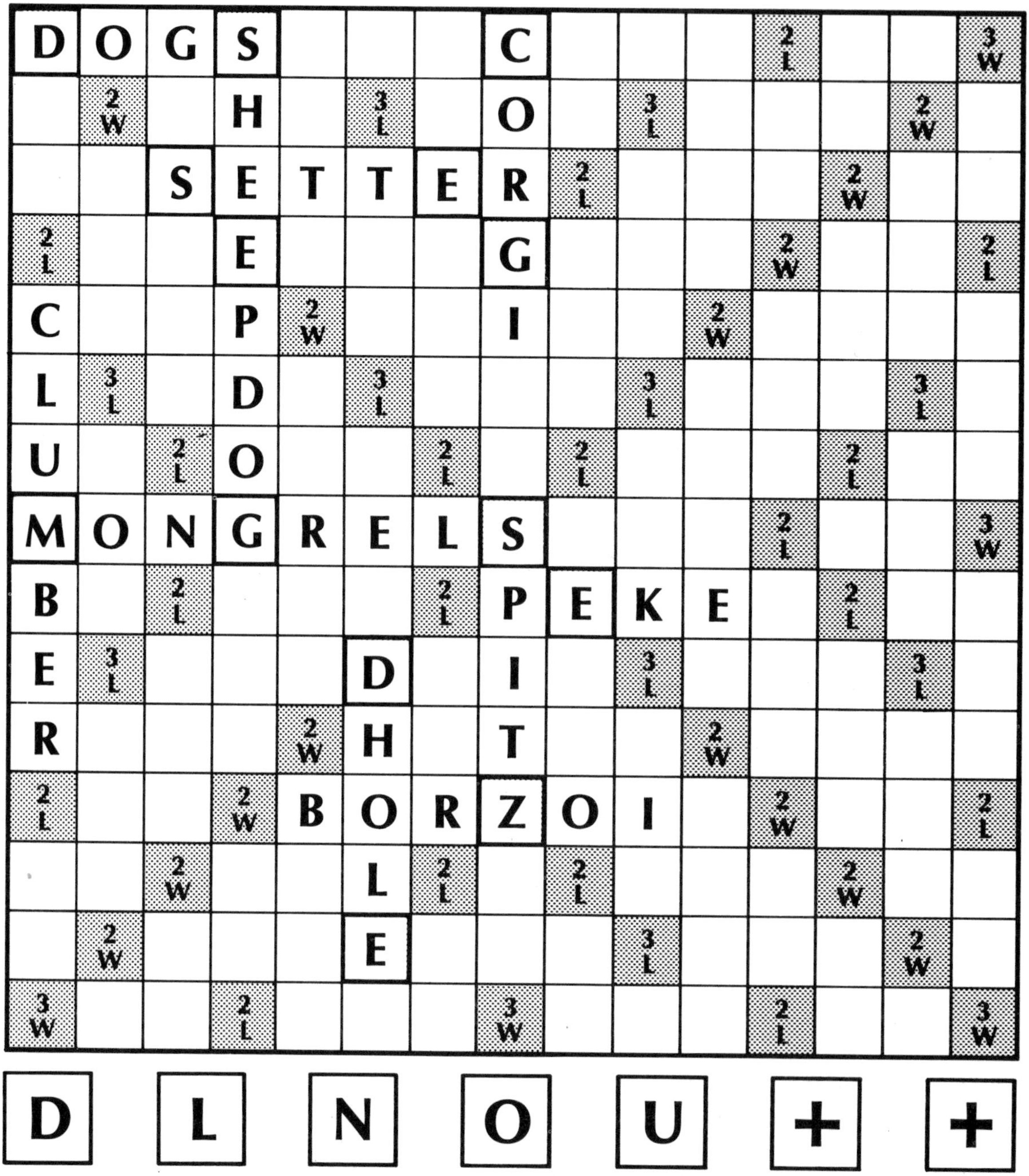
DOGS
SHEEPDOG
CORGI
SETTER
CLUMBER
MONGRELS
SPITZ
PEKE
DHOLE
BORZOI
D L N O U + +

# 5. Es ONLY

Forget definitions. The theme here is that E is the only vowel allowed to appear. Even if you use the blank, it must be either as an E or as a consonant.

| 1 | 2 | 3 | 4 | 5 | 6 | 7 | 8 | 9 | 10 | 11 | 12 | 13 | 14 | 15 |
|---|---|---|---|---|---|---|---|---|----|----|----|----|----|----|
| 3W | | | 2L | | | 3W | | | | | 2L | | | 3W |
| | 2W | | | 3L | | | | 3L | | | | 2W | | |
| | | 2W | | | 2L | | 2L | | | | 2W | | | |
| 2L | | | 2W | | | 2L | | | | | 2W | | | 2L |
| | | | 2W | | | | | 2W | | | P | | | |
| | 3L | | | 3L | | | | 3L | | P | E | L | F | |
| | | 2L | | | 2L | | K | 2L | S | 2L | N | | R | |
| 3W | | | 2L | | | | E | N | T | E | N | T | E | S |
| | | 2L | | | 2L | | R | 2L | R | | E | M | E | |
| | 3L | | | 3L | | | B | L | E | N | D | | D | |
| | | | 2W | | | | | | N | 2W | | | | |
| 2L | | | 2L | | | | | | G | 2W | | | | 2L |
| | | 2W | N | | | C | R | W | T | H | | 2W | | |
| | 2W | | T | 3L | W | | | + | | | | 2W | | |
| 3W | | S | C | H | E | M | E | R | S | | 2L | | | 3W |

Rack: **E  E  E  E  G  X  +**

## 6. FISH

Things fishy are required here. The names of fish and other aquatic creatures are all that's allowed in this puzzle.

Letter tiles: **A  E  H  R  S  T  +**

# 7. GAMES

Perhaps Scrabble players don't know any games other than Scrabble. In which case they'll have a tough time with this puzzle, for all words played are the names of games or sports. But don't look for SCRABBLE; it's not there!

Rack tiles: A I N O S + +

## 8. NAMES

The name of the game here is names – personal forenames. All of the words in this puzzle are male and female forenames. But each one appears in *Chambers Twentieth Century Dictionary*.

## 9. Os ONLY

Ooooo! No definitions are involved here. Just make sure that O is the only vowel to appear in this puzzle.

|     |     |     |     |     |     |     |     |     |     |     |     |     |     |     |
|-----|-----|-----|-----|-----|-----|-----|-----|-----|-----|-----|-----|-----|-----|-----|
| 3W  |     |     | 2L  |     |     | 3W  |     |     |     | 2L  |     |     |     | 3W  |
|     | 2W  |     |     |     | F   |     |     | 3L  |     |     |     |     | 2W  |     |
|     |     | 2W  |     |     | R   | 2L  |     | 2L  |     |     | 2W  |     |     |     |
| 2L  |     |     | W   | R   | O   | N   | G   | S   |     |     | 2W  |     |     | 2L  |
|     |     | P   |     | 2W  | N   |     | C   |     | 2W  |     |     |     |     |     |
|     | 3L  | R   |     | D   |     | H   | 3L  |     |     |     |     | 3L  |     |     |
|     | B   | O   | N   | D   | S   | 2L  | L   |     |     | T   | 2L  |     |     |     |
| 3W  |     | M   | 2L  |     | G   | R   | O   | W   | T   | H   |     |     | 3W  |     |
|     |     | P   |     |     | 2L  | C   |     |     | R   | 2L  |     |     |     |     |
|     | 3L  | T   |     | J   |     | K   | 3L  |     | O   | X   | 3L  |     |     |     |
|     |     |     | T   | O   | M   | B   | S   |     | 2W  | N   |     |     |     |     |
| 2L  |     | V   |     | L   |     | 2L  |     |     | G   |     |     |     | 2L  |     |
|     | F   | R   | O   | N   | T   | 2L  |     | 2L  |     |     | 2W  |     |     |     |
|     | 2W  |     | L   |     | 3L  |     |     | 3L  |     |     |     | 2W  |     |     |
| 3W  |     | T   |     |     |     | 3W  |     |     | 2L  |     |     |     | 3W  |     |

| D | L | N | O | O | S | Z |

101

## 10. VEGETABLES

MARROW, COURGETTE, ZUCCHINI, ENDIVE and GARLIC are likely candidates to appear in this game. Vegetables, herbs and spices are the only items permitted here.

| | | | | | | | | | | | | | | |
|---|---|---|---|---|---|---|---|---|---|---|---|---|---|---|
| 3W | | | 2L | | | | 3W | | | | 2L | | | 3W |
| | 2W | | | | 3L | | | | 3L | | | | 2W | |
| | | 2W | | | | 2L | | 2L | | | | 2W | | |
| 2L | | | 2W | | | | G | | | | 2W | | | 2L |
| | | | | 2W | | | H | | | T | | | B | |
| | 3L | | | | B | | E | | 3L | U | | | E | |
| | | 2L | | | E | 2L | R | 2L | | R | | 2L | A | |
| 3W | | | 2L | L | E | E | K | | O | N | I | O | N | 3W |
| | | 2L | | | T | 2L | I | 2L | | I | | 2L | | |
| | 3L | | Y | | R | | N | E | E | P | | | 3L | |
| P | O | T | A | T | O | | | | | 2W | | | | |
| 2L | | | M | | O | R | A | C | H | E | 2W | | | 2L |
| | | 2W | | | T | 2L | | O | | | | 2W | | |
| | 2W | | | | 3L | | | S | 3L | | | | 2W | |
| 3W | | | 2L | | | | 3W | | | | 2L | | | 3W |

A C L O R Y Z

# 6

# SCRABBLE
# CHALLENGES

# HUNDREDS OF ANAGRAMS

The 50-point bonus for playing all seven of your tiles in one turn is the key to high scoring in Scrabble. Get two, three or even four of these bonuses in a game and you are well on your way to achieving that big score. But you do need practice when it comes to juggling the seven tiles on your rack. After all, if you have seven different letters, and none is a blank, there are 5,040 different ways to arrange the letters. You don't have the time, and your opponent won't have the patience, for you to go methodically through them all. You've got to be able to take short cuts. Of course, if one of your tiles is a blank, or you are trying to use one of several letters already on the board, the number of possible letter combinations increases dramatically. Here it is even more necessary to be able to take short cuts.

What sort of short cuts are there when it comes to looking for words? First of all, look for common letter groups, Like -ATE, DIS-, -ED, -ER, -EST, -GHT, -IER, -IES, -ING, -ION, -ORY, -OUS, OUT-, OVER-, PRO-, -TCH and UN-. Secondly, keep an eye out for pairs of letters that often go together, like BL-, CR-, DR-, FL-, GR-, -MM-, -NN-, SP-, TH-, WH- and so on. Know which letters don't usually come together, for example BG, CW, DP, FK, GW, HR, MG, SG. Thirdly, try to make a three-letter word and a four-letter word out of your seven letters. It's amazing how often words like BULLDOG, CATSUIT, DAYTIME, and EGGCUPS can be overlooked when you are concentrating solely on making a seven-letter word. These are the sorts of words with which even accomplished Scrabble players have difficulty.

So, to get you really into the swing of looking for seven-letter words, here are 500 (yes, 500!) racks of seven letters. They have been arranged into five groups of 100, each group involving progressively higher-scoring letters, and more of them. Every set of seven letters can be rearranged to give a genuine seven-letter word. There may be a few cases where more than one word can be made, but not many. All words can be found in the 1983 edition of *Chambers Twentieth Century Dictionary*. Most of the words can also be found in *The Official Scrabble Players Dictionary*.

# 100 ANAGRAMS

Here are 100 racks of seven letters, every letter being worth just
a single point. Can you find the words that these letters make?

| | | | |
|---|---|---|---|
| 1. SEATEAR | 26. SEATIRE | 51. EARTOES | 76. USETEAR |
| 2. ELLRAIN | 27. ANISLER | 52. AIRSALE | 77. IRESALE |
| 3. EARTILE | 28. ALLRITE | 53. ALITTER | 78. LIEURAT |
| 4. AILSITE | 29. ILLSEAT | 54. OILSEAT | 79. INASORE |
| 5. NEARSIR | 30. RAINTIE | 55. RAINNET | 80. RAINTOE |
| 6. INTEASE | 31. ANISEIT | 56. OATSINE | 81. AIRSEAT |
| 7. AIRTIES | 32. AIRTOES | 57. ALANERS | 82. LENSRAN |
| 8. EARNSLO | 33. LARNESS | 58. NANTLER | 83. LATTERN |
| 9. RENAULT | 34. ANTSALE | 59. ENSLANT | 84. LOANEST |
| 10. LUNATES | 35. RATSOLE | 60. LURATES | 85. RANSENT |
| 11. EARROTS | 36. SEETIRE | 61. TIRESET | 86. NESTLER |
| 12. RETNESS | 37. SETLINE | 62. TINLENS | 87. LIENIST |
| 13. LISTNER | 38. ROTTIES | 63. SELLROT | 88. SLOTTER |
| 14. LENSROT | 39. SORETON | 64. ERRTONS | 89. RUTLENS |
| 15. ENTRUSS | 40. UREATEA | 65. ASEAANT | 90. SEASAIL |
| 16. RATALIA | 41. TENAEON | 66. OLEAREA | 91. AIRTEAT |
| 17. EATSTEN | 42. REALOAR | 67. EUROALA | 92. SUEREAR |
| 18. NEARTAR | 43. RARERAS | 68. LASTAIR | 93. NEEILEA |
| 19. SEALORE | 44. SEATIES | 69. RANLEER | 94. ILASSIE |
| 20. LOANITE | 45. LUNAITE | 70. SANEINN | 95. ANTINEO |
| 21. NOASIES | 46. AUTISTE | 71. ONERALL | 96. ALLTENT |
| 22. ALLSORE | 47. TEALULU | 72. OURALEU | 97. ENNAUTO |
| 23. URASSES | 48. STANNET | 73. LEENTIT | 98. TERRANT |
| 24. UNRATER | 49. REULISE | 74. UTUREAS | 99. ALLINON |
| 25. LIRIONS | 50. OUTSUNE | 75. UNTONER | 100. UNROLES |

# ANOTHER 100 ANAGRAMS

Here are another 100 racks of seven letters. Each rack has letters worth one and two points. Can you rearrange each of the sets of letters to find a genuine word?

| | | | |
|---|---|---|---|
| 1. SNEDDER | 26. LIDSAGE | 51. TEASIDE | 76. GEENAIL |
| 2. EAUINGS | 27. REDSAND | 52. AEROING | 77. OLADIES |
| 3. RADLETS | 28. ASINEGG | 53. SLANGLE | 78. LENSGAG |
| 4. ADINASE | 29. RENODES | 54. REDANTS | 79. ASATING |
| 5. INGRANT | 30. DIRESTS | 55. GRASING | 80. TEELING |
| 6. DANGIES | 31. SEERING | 56. INRENDS | 81. GLINLET |
| 7. RANTRIG | 32. INGRUTE | 57. NOTIGER | 82. TINGIES |
| 8. DUNSIER | 33. RAGLENS | 58. SITAGED | 83. GRANTIT |
| 9. ANTLEGS | 34. ADDSINE | 59. GASLENS | 84. AGREING |
| 10. AURIDES | 35. STRAGLE | 60. GREENDS | 85. DEANIES |
| 11. AUTIDES | 36. GANITOR | 61. INTOLEG | 86. SNERRED |
| 12. LESSING | 37. LITRANG | 62. GOTTROD | 87. SNIRTED |
| 13. SEAINGS | 38. GRANNIS | 63. INGLUSE | 88. DIRTERS |
| 14. TAGIONS | 39. UNGLITE | 64. RINDIES | 89. TUESING |
| 15. NESTLID | 40. NEONTAG | 65. GONDOSS | 90. DERAGED |
| 16. OURSUDA | 41. GALLLIE | 66. DISNUTS | 91. TINGODS |
| 17. GLESSED | 42. DUSSAGE | 67. OGREIDE | 92. ALARGUN |
| 18. TOEAGES | 43. DUOTEAT | 68. GGADDER | 93. ALONGDO |
| 19. DOLTAGE | 44. TILEDAD | 69. DETRATE | 94. NEOGGOD |
| 20. DUTIDEA | 45. DUOROOT | 70. GOALLER | 95. DILLGUN |
| 21. SNURTED | 46. LORINDA | 71. SEAGODS | 96. ITSDUGS |
| 22. SANDDEE | 47. TELDEED | 72. ATGLASS | 97. UNLODES |
| 23. AEIOUDL | 48. INGGGOD | 73. DADGING | 98. ESSRAGS |
| 24. AEIOUGL | 49. GETSTEA | 74. LEGDEAL | 99. LUDDITE |
| 25. UNAITED | 50. OUTRAID | 75. DISRING | 100. IDEANOD |

# A FURTHER 100 ANAGRAMS

Another 100 racks of seven letters. This time, the point values of the letters involved are one, two, three and four, so you can expect to find every letter except J, K, Q, X and Z.

| | | | |
|---|---|---|---|
| 1. MEDIATS | 26. REPTILA | 51. NEBLAGS | 76. GANDIPS |
| 2. GARNISM | 27. TINBAGS | 52. REDCANS | 77. SELFNAG |
| 3. DEARISH | 28. TARFIES | 53. RIMLETS | 78. LEADISH |
| 4. VANSIRE | 29. BINCRAG | 54. SWANLEG | 79. BANGIER |
| 5. AGINSOP | 30. ENRICAL | 55. SANSPIG | 80. GINCASE |
| 6. BRANITE | 31. GLENISM | 56. VANLIER | 81. IVANGEL |
| 7. CRENSED | 32. SPRANED | 57. ANYGITS | 82. BADLIES |
| 8. BIGLENS | 33. FREENDS | 58. CURTENS | 83. NERVEDS |
| 9. RENEWTS | 34. GINTAPS | 59. HAGLINE | 84. DERMENS |
| 10. DRENSHE | 35. TENBRAS | 60. GLIBNET | 85. IMANGLE |
| 11. SERBEND | 36. LIPREAS | 61. ANCORGI | 86. LENGIFT |
| 12. EEWARTS | 37. SELFRAN | 62. ELFGINS | 87. SINGBRA |
| 13. GLIMENT | 38. YINGERS | 63. EARPETS | 88. SELFART |
| 14. SUNTERM | 39. PEERIST | 64. GNAWIER | 89. TRAYING |
| 15. BARLIES | 40. FAGTINS | 65. ACORSET | 90. VENGIST |
| 16. SPAINER | 41. TINGEMS | 66. HAGBINS | 91. ENPORTS |
| 17. SILVENT | 42. BLANTER | 67. SEVIRAL | 92. VANLETS |
| 18. SINSHAG | 43. POLTERS | 68. RESTLAW | 93. LADYIES |
| 19. BITHERS | 44. PANGIER | 69. GINVATS | 94. REDPENS |
| 20. BIGNETS | 45. LABTIRE | 70. ENWARTS | 95. IREHANG |
| 21. BESTIER | 46. LAWRISE | 71. ROBENTS | 96. UNISHAG |
| 22. RANCELT | 47. ENDRIPS | 72. LEGPANS | 97. ABITERS |
| 23. ACIDEST | 48. UPSAGIN | 73. MINGERS | 98. SADEVIL |
| 24. SLARPEN | 49. GRINCES | 74. NVARLET | 99. TUSHIER |
| 25. VANSIDE | 50. TIRELAY | 75. FANGIER | 100. PINGLET |

# YET ANOTHER 100 ANAGRAMS

The 100 racks of seven letters here all incorporate one of the five high-scoring letters, J, K, Q, X and Z. All the other letters in these racks are one or two-point letters. Can you find all 100 of the words?

| | | | |
|---|---|---|---|
| 1. LIEJARS | 26. TANZELS | 51. JETAIDE | 76. ADQUART |
| 2. DISKANE | 27. LARQUER | 52. RAGKNIT | 77. OXTURES |
| 3. ZESTIAL | 28. REKNOTS | 53. SLANZER | 78. DISTREK |
| 4. SNARKED | 29. SLEZING | 54. DISDIKE | 79. NAKITES |
| 5. INKTREE | 30. NAZEIST | 55. TELKING | 80. TANKIER |
| 6. JETLING | 31. GANXIST | 56. TRONKET | 81. JAGLENS |
| 7. LARSAUK | 32. ELKSRAN | 57. DISLAKE | 82. TAJNESS |
| 8. LESKING | 33. STROJEL | 58. INRAKES | 83. SINGJET |
| 9. JERGLIN | 34. SNARZED | 59. TANQUEN | 84. KLANETS |
| 10. GINKOTS | 35. LEGJINS | 60. REALKIN | 85. NODJIER |
| 11. SKRINED | 36. DELANKS | 61. SARLIKE | 86. LEKTERS |
| 12. JANEIST | 37. REXNEST | 62. TENTKID | 87. TALKIEO |
| 13. GISNAKE | 38. SNERZED | 63. INDOTAJ | 88. LEOTIZE |
| 14. JARGNEL | 39. RQUANTA | 64. NOTADZE | 89. GJUTINT |
| 15. SINKIES | 40. TRIJEST | 65. SUQROTA | 90. SLENKOE |
| 16. TAXIINE | 41. INDOJET | 66. EXILALA | 91. TROJANI |
| 17. ONESKET | 42. DRANKER | 67. ASIASUQ | 92. OKINESS |
| 18. LIQUANT | 43. EATAXER | 68. NOTOIZE | 93. ROLLIZE |
| 19. DEALTEX | 44. EUTAXED | 69. QUIRTLE | 94. SEXARIA |
| 20. GRINRAJ | 45. NINIQUE | 70. DOAXIER | 95. TRAQUET |
| 21. TOAZIES | 46. SUEQUIT | 71. LUZTONE | 96. SEXOIRS |
| 22. TOOLIZE | 47. TANLAZE | 72. URATIZE | 97. TIJUANE |
| 23. ARRQUET | 48. TOIZIES | 73. TINTJOG | 98. TEQUINE |
| 24. DUROJAN | 49. TRIQUOT | 74. LOGTASK | 99. URALJUG |
| 25. REAXEED | 50. EXETING | 75. TEENSEX | 100. TEENREX |

# THE LAST 100 ANAGRAMS

Another 100 racks of seven letters for you to wrestle with! This time, all the racks involve a good mixture of low-scoring, middle-scoring and high-scoring letters. How quickly can you find the hidden words?

| | | | |
|---|---|---|---|
| 1. MINKDOG | 26. NICKQUE | 51. ZONELEG | 76. YOLTRAY |
| 2. FYMITYS | 27. BIGNIBF | 52. NAFFHOD | 77. KIMGIMC |
| 3. HAHAPNT | 28. BEVORRP | 53. JOKILLY | 78. CIDILLY |
| 4. ZOGRANA | 29. BEZALEM | 54. TUQUMAN | 79. MILIHUT |
| 5. FLUTZES | 30. CAUFISH | 55. RINIQUY | 80. OXTAVER |
| 6. BIZTUBK | 31. MIDIFEW | 56. YUNTCHE | 81. NAPHLAX |
| 7. MANGYST | 32. COOLHAL | 57. MUSTISH | 82. WOLLYEY |
| 8. HERKING | 33. TIFFAMS | 58. CONTOGA | 83. LEEKYHO |
| 9. PODLYOW | 34. THLYNGE | 59. FIZNICY | 84. QUOXINE |
| 10. HARBBUR | 35. FLOOHEX | 60. CRYROKE | 85. YEHEING |
| 11. GLOOOZY | 36. CAPHRIG | 61. MUMUGWP | 86. FLIQUEY |
| 12. OXBOWDO | 37. DAMPIRY | 62. FANNYIC | 87. VELTYNO |
| 13. DELXIFY | 38. CLOOGEY | 63. SAYLAMB | 88. OXENHAG |
| 14. ONLYGUY | 39. SWANCRY | 64. ITMOVED | 89. DOZENBR |
| 15. HUCOUNT | 40. ESQUICE | 65. FORFANS | 90. HAMYAKS |
| 16. DACKJAW | 41. THYFRIT | 66. HOLIBAN | 91. ALFBUSH |
| 17. DYENOSK | 42. ZEEPART | 67. HARNTAX | 92. DANKYEL |
| 18. ACCANVY | 43. FREDDAW | 68. HOTDIPY | 93. MANYLOW |
| 19. DEARPUG | 44. LIQUONJ | 69. HITWISH | 94. KLAYJAW |
| 20. MCBOXCO | 45. ANTYSYD | 70. WHADIER | 95. BBLIQUE |
| 21. FIJYTUS | 46. TAIVERY | 71. MYSTOMP | 96. BOORHUG |
| 22. NUTSPEW | 47. CROMADZ | 72. NYRANTY | 97. DRKWAWA |
| 23. WHOSDAY | 48. MYNAZIS | 73. LEXYCAT | 98. GLOUNDY |
| 24. GINNWAY | 49. ZIRCLAY | 74. THRAWPA | 99. WRONKET |
| 25. COOLVAN | 50. HAYWHIG | 75. KRAWWOX | 100. FIGSHOD |

# EIGHT EIGHTS

What is the highest score that you can make from eight moves
by playing seven letters at a time and filling the squares
indicated in the diagram on the facing page? Your solution must
be restricted to using letters no more often than they appear in
the usual distribution of 100 Scrabble tiles. For example, you
may only use a Z once, a V twice, a G three times, and so on.

This puzzle was devised by Ron Jerome, of Bracknell,
Berkshire, England, and originally appeared in Allan Simmons'
magazine *Onwords*, the Scrabble enthusiasts' magazine. In the
example shown below, the total score comes to 617 points, and
uses these words:

| | | | |
|---|---|---|---|
| SPENDING | 92 points | BRISTLED | 72 points |
| SANDARAC | 76 points | CHOLIAMB | 77 points |
| RELIGION | 70 points | LAVATORY | 66 points |
| MAGNESIA | 78 points | IRONWARE | 86 points |

Of course, you can do better than this, can't you?

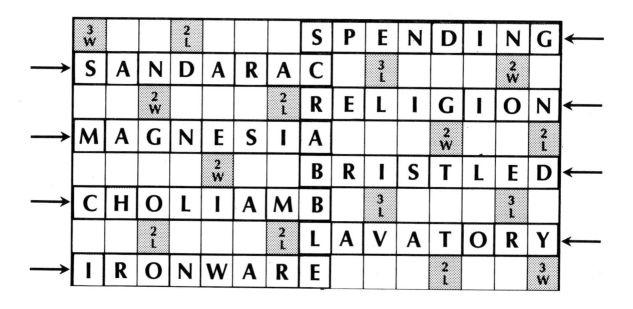

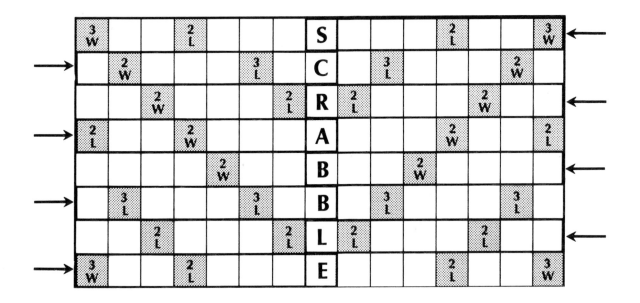

## IMPROPER NAMES

The next time you get the opportunity, put a word like AFGHAN or SWEDE on the board, and listen to the howls of protest as your opponent insists that proper names are not permitted in Scrabble. Both AFGHAN and SWEDE are allowed – an afghan is a kind of woollen blanket, and a swede is a type of turnip, or rutabaga as Americans would have it. There are dozens of words that you might think ought to begin with a capital letter but which can be spelled with a lower-case initial letter. Here are 50 definitions of such words, words which, according to both *The Official Scrabble Players Dictionary* and the 1983 edition of *Chambers*, can all be used in Scrabble because they can begin with a small initial letter. See if you can think of the words to go with the definitions.

1. inspiring reverence
2. a type of carriage
3. a card game
4. a hot pepper
5. fine porcelain ware
6. with each person paying for him- or herself
7. a wind or storm from the east
8. a container for heating liquids
9. a large kangaroo
10. a unit of electricity
11. a loaded die
12. a liquor
13. an elaborate dance
14. a halo
15. a woollen shirt
16. to break up and level soil
17. a unit of inductance
18. a cotton fabric
19. a long poem
20. to coat with glossy, black lacquer
21. a knitted shirt
22. a unit of temperature
23. knew
24. a bean
25. a condition of neglect
26. a humorous verse
27. a friction match
28. something remarkable
29. a raincoat
30. an alcoholic beverage
31. soft leather
32. a wrestling hold
33. a unit of force
34. peaceful
35. a unit of radiation dosage
36. a metrical narrative
37. to put a definite end to
38. a concave moulding
39. a water-pipe with a connection for two hoses
40. a light carriage
41. the uppermost structure on a steamboat
42. a soft, friable rock
43. a long, loose overcoat
44. a short friction match
45. a mineral
46. marks with welts

47. to fail to pay a debt
48. the effect of pollen on certain plant structures
49. to pull suddenly
50. young gentlemen

# MAKE A FEW WORDS

Using the letter distribution of a standard English game of Scrabble, what is the smallest number of words that can be made? All 100 letters must be used, and the two blanks may represent any letters you wish. Hyphenated words are allowed, as are proper names.

When this problem was originally set as a competition in a British games magazine in the early 1970s, the winning solution came from Ron Jerome, of Bracknell, Berkshire, England. His solution used just seven words. All of his words appear in the 1972 edition of *Chambers Twentieth Century Dictionary*. (They all appear in the 1983 edition, too.) His seven words were:

DELIVERY-VANS
EXPERIMENTALIZES
HONORIFICABILITUDINITY
JACK-GO-TO-BED-AT-NOON
QUEEN-OF-THE-MEADOWS
UPSURGE
WARRAGALS

The blanks are used as an N and an S.

Even when other dictionaries are allowed as sources for the words, seven words still seems to be the lowest limit, even though the number of hyphenated words can be reduced. Here is another seven-word solution:

DIOXYDIAMIDOARSENOBENZOL
EQUIPPING
ETHYLENEDIAMINETETRAACETATE
FAVOUR
JUGOSLAVIC
REFURBISH
WESTWARD-LOOKING

The blanks are used as a D and an I.

Can a seven-word solution with no hyphens be found? Can a seven-word solution with no proper names be found? Can solutions with less than seven words be found?

# A NEWS ITEM

On 11 March 1975, *The Times* contained the following item:
'Phoebe Winch of Sherborne thinks she may have invented
a new game. I fear that she may be right, and that it could
prove compulsive. It is to compose something sensible
using all the letter tiles supplied with Scrabble and using no
other letters. Her own best effort is: "I AM DIETING. I EAT
QUINCE JELLY. LOTS OF GROUND MAIZE GIVES
VARIETY. I COOK RHUBARB AND SODA, WEEP ANEW,
OR PUT ON EXTRA FLESH." Mrs Winch says that she is
not satisfied with the result. I expect some of you can do
better.'

Can you do better? It appears that Mrs Winch has decided to
ignore the blanks. This suggests two versions of the game:

(i) excluding the blanks, and using the other 98 letters
(ii) using the blanks as any letters you wish, along with the
other 98 letters.

See if you can do better than:

I WAS THE JUST QUEEN OF AN EMPIRE. I GAZED ON
BRITAIN. I HAVE RULED SO LONG. SO I EXPECTED
LOYALTY BACK. I FAVOURED NOT GRIM WAR.

That's 98 letters, with the two blanks excluded.
Here are two sentences which use all 100 tiles. In the first
sentence, the blanks are used as an N and an S:

THE ZEBRAS ARE BOUNDING TOO ANXIOUSLY
ALONGSIDE MILES OF QUICK FLOWING RIVER WATER
JUST TO EVADE PAINTED PEA MACHINERY.

In the second sentence, both the blanks are used as Ds:

HOWEVER DID PAVID BODIES FIND TIME TO ENJOY
AN EXERCISE, USING ALL TILES, MAKING UP QUEER
WORDS FOR A TALE ABOUT A CRAZY THING.

That second sentence seems to have more than just a remote
connection with Scrabble!

# 7

# A
# PUZZLING
# POT POURRI

A pot pourri was originally a mixed stew or hash of meat and vegetables, but can now be applied to a collection of unconnected or only vaguely related parts, whether they have anything to do with food or not. 'Pourri' means 'rotten' in French, and comes from the verb 'pourrir', to rot.

This pot pourri section contains 70 different quizzes, queries and questions. Some are trivially easy and can be solved in seconds; others are likely to prove extremely time-consuming. None, I trust, is rotten! Various solutions are offered at the end of the book, but these may not necessarily be the best ones possible. You may well be able to improve on the solutions given. If so, well done!

**1.**

The six letters EEIRST can be combined with the letter A to make a seven-letter word, SERIATE. The same letters can be combined with a B to make another seven-letter word, REBITES. And so on, with a variety of different letters. In fact, EEIRST can be combined separately with 13 different letters of the alphabet to make valid seven-letter words. For example:

| | | | | | |
|---|---|---|---|---|---|
| A | SERIATE | H | HEISTER | P | RESPITE |
| B | REBITES | L | STERILE | R | RETIRES |
| C | RECITES | M | METIERS | T | TESTIER |
| D | DIETERS | N | ENTRIES | V | RESTIVE |
| E | EERIEST | | | | |

Can you find a group of six letters, all different and not including a blank, which will combine separately with over 20 different letters in the same manner?

**2.**

Find an anagram of the word JUG. Of all major dictionaries, the anagram only seems to appear in the 1972 and 1983 editions of *Chambers Twentieth Century Dictionary*.

**3.**

Two anagrams, please, of the letters ADHILOY.

**4.**

Imagine that you are playing a solitaire game of Scrabble. There are only 26 letters in the pool which are available for play. They are A to Z, and they must be taken from the pool in strict alphabetical sequence. Is it possible to use all 26 letters on the board? What is the highest score obtainable? Any unused letters must be deducted from your total score.

For example, the first rack is ABCDEFG. If you played FACED as your first word, you would have BG left, so your next rack of seven letters would be BGHIJKL. In the diagram shown here, the following moves have been made in an attempt to use all 26 letters. You can almost certainly do better.

| 1 | 2 | 3 | 4 | 5 | 6 | 7 | 8 | 9 | 10 | 11 | 12 | 13 | 14 | 15 |
|---|---|---|---|---|---|---|---|---|----|----|----|----|----|----|
| 3W |  |  | 2L |  |  |  | 3W |  |  |  | 2L |  |  | 3W |
|  | 2W |  |  |  | 3L |  |  |  | 3L |  |  |  | 2W |  |
|  |  | 2W |  |  |  | 2L |  | 2L |  |  |  | 2W |  |  |
| 2L |  |  | 2W |  |  |  | S |  |  |  | 2W |  |  | 2L |
|  |  |  |  | 2W |  |  | Q |  |  | 2W |  |  |  |  |
|  | 3L |  |  |  | 3L |  | U |  | 3L | V |  |  | 3L |  |
|  |  | 2L |  | J |  | B | I | N | G | O |  | 2L |  |  |
| 3W |  |  | F | A | C | E | D |  |  | W | 2L |  |  | 3W |
|  |  | 2L |  | K |  | L |  | 2L |  |  |  | 2L |  |  |
|  | 3L |  |  |  | 3L | T |  |  | 3L |  |  |  | 3L |  |
|  |  |  |  | 2W |  |  |  |  |  | 2W |  |  |  |  |
| 2L |  |  | 2W |  |  |  | 2L |  |  |  | 2W |  |  | 2L |
|  |  | 2W |  |  |  | 2L |  | 2L |  |  |  | 2W |  |  |
|  | 2W |  |  |  | 3L |  |  |  | 3L |  |  |  | 2W |  |
| 3W |  |  | 2L |  |  |  | 3W |  |  |  | 2L |  |  | 3W |

| | |
|---|---|
| 1. FACED | 30 |
| 2. JAK | 14 |
| 3. ID | 3 |
| 4. BINGO, BE | 19 |
| 5. QUID | 14 |
| 6. SQUID | 16 |
| 7. BELT | 7 |
| 8. VOW | 9 |
| minus unused letters | −26 |
| Total | 86 |

**5.**
What three-letter word can be added to the most different, single letters to form four-letter words?

**6.**
Four anagrams, please, of the letters BDEORTU.

**7.**
IMRSSTU. No As, no Es, no Os – and yet two anagrams. What are they?

**8.**
What is the largest rectangle of letters that can be constructed from a series of legitimate moves? There must be no spaces between the letters.

**9.**
What group of six letters, one of which must be the J, but excluding blanks, combines with the greatest number of letters of the alphabet to produce valid seven-letter words?

**10.**
Find three seven-letter words, each of which contains the five vowels AEIOU.

**11.**
Eight eight-letter words, please, each of which contains the vowels AEIOU.

**12.**
You are playing an idealized solitaire game of Scrabble. The letters can be selected from the pool in any order you wish. If the only vowel allowed in this game is A, what is the highest score possible? You may not play any Es, Is, Os, Us and Ys. If you play any blanks, they must be As or consonants. Do not deduct the value of any unplayed tiles. Try aiming for well over 1,000 points.

**13.**
AEGILNT has four anagrams. What are they?

**14.**
Find a seven-letter word whose letters are all in the first half of the alphabet (A to M, inclusive).

**15.**
This is a very simple question, but it will take some time to come up with a high-scoring solution. Playing seven letters at a time (except for the last turn), what is the highest idealized solitaire score possible?

**16.**
Reduce every seven-letter word to its 'alphabetically reduced' form; in other words, list the letters which make up the word in alphabetical order. For example, SEATING becomes AEGINST, and MAGNIFY becomes AFGIMNY. These are the alphabetically reduced forms. Now sort all these alphabetically reduced forms into strict alphabetical order. For example, AEGINST would come before AFGIMNY. What is the very first one, and what word has created it? And what is the very last one, and what word has created it? Remember, just seven-letter words.

**17.**
What three seven-letter words can be made from the letters EARLIMB?

**18.**
Find a seven-letter word whose letters are all in the second half of the alphabet (N to Z, inclusive).

**19.**

Can you fit all 100 Scrabble tiles into an 11-by-11 grid crossword-fashion so that all words are interlocked? It doesn't matter whether your solution possesses symmetry. An 11-by-11 square has a total area of 121 squares. Is a smaller rectangle possible? Perhaps 10-by-12, 10-by-11, or 9-by-12?

**20.**

Find seven-letter anagrams for each of these 26 sequences of letters:

| | | | |
|---|---|---|---|
| AJEXBUM | PYXHAYS | FOXPITS | WHIPLUR |
| BIDWANK | DRINKOV | SIRPYKS | HILLYPO |
| SONFINK | ICUMISH | TRYSHAG | DAMNQUO |
| THYRAIN | CLAYMIG | MYCHEAT | HOPIDIX |
| HOWWILT | SNARCCH | CURFLOP | CAHHTTT |
| HINCZAR | TRAVIXU | USMOONY | POXHEAD |
| IMPCHYN | HANKDAY | | |

**21.**

What is the highest score it is possible to gain by playing a single Q? You may need to consider the list of words elsewhere in this book that have a Q not followed by a U. Or you may not . . .

**22.**

Find an eight-letter word whose letters are all in the first half of the alphabet (A to M, inclusive).

**23.**

There are three anagrams of the letters ACEEMRT. What are they?

**24.**

In a game of Scrabble where changing tiles is not permitted, what is the lowest possible final score for both players?

**25.**

The six letters ACEHRS can be combined with 17 separate letters of the alphabet to form seven-letter words. Find examples for each of the 17 groups.

**26.**
You are playing an idealized solitaire game of Scrabble. The letters can be selected from the pool in any order you wish. If the only vowel allowed in this game is E, what is the highest score possible? You may not play any As, Is, Os, Us and Ys. If you play any blanks, they must be Es or consonants. Do not deduct the value of any unplayed tiles. Try aiming for well over 1,000 points.

**27.**
Here are a dozen British placenames. Each can be anagrammed to give a valid Scrabble word. Find all 12.

| | | | |
|---|---|---|---|
| ARUNDEL | CARDIGAN | CHESTER | LANCASTER |
| ATHLONE | CARNOUSTIE | DORSET | MAIDSTONE |
| CAITHNESS | CHELSEA | HASTINGS | WORTHING |

**28.**
Find a nine-letter word whose letters are all in the first half of the alphabet (A to M, inclusive).

**29.**
The idea of alphabetically reduced forms was raised in question 16. Staying with this idea, what is the first alphabetically reduced form beginning with B, and what word generates it? What is the first one beginning with C? And D? And so on through to N?

**30.**
Can you find a group of six letters, all different and not including a blank, which will combine with 20 other separate letters of the alphabet, including J, K, V and Z, to make seven-letter words?

**31.**
Devise an idealized board situation in which the playing of a two-letter word gives the highest score possible. Note that this problem relates to the playing of a *two-letter word*, and not to the playing of two letters!

**32.**
What group of six letters, one of which must be the Q, but excluding blanks, combines with the greatest number of letters of the alphabet to produce valid seven-letter words?

**33.**
Find an eight-letter word whose letters are all in the second half of the alphabet (N to Z, inclusive).

**34.**
ACCEPT is a six-letter word whose letters are arranged in alphabetical order. Can you find a common seven-letter word with its letters in alphabetical order?

**35.**
What two seven-letter words can be made from the letters AEILMNP?

**36.**
Question 29 asked for the first alphabetically reduced form beginning with each of the letters from B to N. Conversely, what are the *last* alphabetically reduced forms beginning with the letters A to N?

**37.**
Find three anagrams of the letters EHISTTW.

**38.**
The order of letters on a typewriter keyboard is QWERTYUIOPASDFGHJKLZXCVBNM. What is the longest common word with its letters in 'typewriter order'? Oddly enough, the answer is also one of the answers to another of these pot pourri questions!

**39.**
Find a ten-letter word whose letters are all in the first half of the alphabet (A to M, inclusive).

**40.**
You are playing an idealized solitaire game of Scrabble. The letters can be selected from the pool in any order you wish. If the only vowel allowed in this game is I, what is the highest score possible? You may not play any As, Es, Os, Us and Ys at all. If you play any blanks, they must either be Is or consonants. Do not deduct the value of any unplayed tiles. Try aiming for over 1,000 points.

**41.**
Find four four-letter words, one beginning with a J, one with J as its second letter, one with J as its third letter, and one with J as its last letter. Find five five-letter words with J in each position, too.

**42.**
ADMNOOR. Two seven-letter words can be formed from these letters. What are they?

**43.**
One letter different from the last question. What two seven-letter words can be made from the letters AADMNOR?

**44.**
Find a nine-letter word whose letters are all in the second half of the alphabet (N to Z, inclusive).

**45.**
IZARD is a five-letter word which can be preceded by L, R, V or W to make a valid six-letter word: LIZARD, RIZARD, VIZARD or WIZARD. Find another five-letter word which can be preceded by L, R, V or W to form a six-letter word.

**46.**
Find four four-letter words, with X in each position. Find five five-letter words, with X in each position.

**47.**
Find three anagrams of the seven letters AHIRSTT.

**48.**

From the letters AEGLPRU, it is fairly easy to find the seven-letter word PLAGUER, which appears in some dictionaries. But can you make another seven-letter word using these letters?

**49.**

Find the seven anagrams of the letters DEIORST.

**50.**

The six letters ADNOPR can be combined with each of the five vowels A, E, I, O and U to form valid seven-letter words. What are they?

**51.**

Here are 13 country names. Each can be anagrammed to give a valid Scrabble word. Find all 13.

| | | | |
|---|---|---|---|
| ALGERIA | CYPRUS | ITALY | PALESTINE |
| ANGOLA | ICELAND | NEPAL | SURINAM |
| BURMA | ISRAEL | NIGER | YEMEN |
| CRETE | | | |

**52.**

On the facing page is an arrangement of 13 letters from which further play is difficult. Indeed, using just *Webster's Third New International Dictionary*, it is not possible to go any further with this board. But switching to the 1983 edition of *Chambers Twentieth Century Dictionary*, it is possible to play on from this position. The difference between the two dictionaries lies in the ways they define the word WUD. *Webster's Third* does not permit the addition of an S, but *Chambers* does. Can you find a similar arrangement of 13 letters from which no further play is possible using *Chambers* and *Webster's Third*?

**53.**

Find four four-letter words, with Z in each position. Find five five-letter words, with Z in each position.

**54.**

You are playing an idealized solitaire game of Scrabble. The letters can be selected from the pool in any order you wish. If the only vowel allowed in this game is O, what is the highest score possible? You may not play any As, Es, Is, Us and Ys at all. If you play any blanks, they must either be Os or consonants. Do not deduct the value of any unplayed tiles. Try aiming for over 1,000 points.

**55.**
The bird's the word! You have just *ten* moves. You must play
only bird names, singular or plural. You can play the same bird
name more than once if you wish. What is the highest total
score you can reach? Remember: no words at all which are not
bird names; and you are restricted to the usual set of 100
Scrabble tiles.

**56.**
Find an 11-letter word whose letters are all in the first half of the
alphabet (A to M, inclusive).

**57.**
Three anagrams are required here from the letters IREGEMS.
What are they?

**58.**
What group of six letters, one of which must be the X, but
excluding blanks, combines with the greatest number of letters
of the alphabet to produce valid seven-letter words?

**59.**
The group of letters AEGLLRY has four anagrams, all extremely
common words. What are they?

**60.**
Can you find a valid Scrabble word of seven letters using the
letters of IRELAND?

**61.**
The alphabetically reduced form of a word is generated by
arranging its letters in alphabetical order. For example,
CARBONS has ABCNORS as its alphabetically reduced form.
Find six seven-letter words whose alphabetically reduced forms
begin ABCDE.

**62.**
Three anagrams for ONEPART are required here. What are they?

**63.**

A six-letter word, please, with *four* Us!

**64.**

The tiles EERST and a blank can be combined separately with all 26 letters of the alphabet, with the blank standing for a variety of letters. Can you find examples for all 26 letters?

**65.**

You are playing an idealized solitaire game of Scrabble. The letters can be selected from the pool in any order you wish. If the only vowel allowed in this game is U, what is the highest score possible? You may not play any As, Es, Is, Os and Ys at all. If you play any blanks, they must be Us or consonants. Do not deduct the value of any unplayed tiles. Try aiming for over 500 points.

**66.**

Find a ten-letter word whose letters are all in the second half of the alphabet (N to Z, inclusive).

**67.**

You are playing a game of Scrabble, and on your rack are the seven tiles EGILNT and a blank. List all the seven-letter words which can be made from these tiles.

**68.**

Find a seven-letter word ending in the two letters GD.

**69.**

Please find four anagrams of these seven letters: EHILOST.

**70.**

What group of six letters, one of which must be the Z, but excluding blanks, combines with the greatest number of letters of the alphabet to produce valid seven-letter words?

# 8

# FOREIGN LANGUAGE SCRABBLE

Scrabble is available in a variety of foreign language editions. There's French, Dutch, Spanish, German, Arabic, Afrikaans, Danish, Finnish, Swedish, Norwegian, Portuguese, Yiddish, Russian, Italian and Greek. Foreign language Scrabble sets tend to have different letter distributions, different point values for the letters, and even varying numbers of letters.

Dutch Scrabble sets have 102 tiles, and the standard 26 letters of the English alphabet are all represented. But the point values and the letter distributions are different to those of the standard English Scrabble. For example, there are 18 Es, 10 Ns and 2 Zs. The solitary F is worth five points, and the Us are each worth four points.

German Scrabble sets have a massive 119 tiles. In addition to the usual English letters, there are also tiles for Ä, Ö and Ü. There are 16 Es, 8 Ss and 2 Zs. The J is worth only six points, the K only three points, and the Y is worth ten points. The strangest feature of German Scrabble, though, is the fact that the game is played with eight tiles at a time on players' racks, and a bonus of 50 points is awarded for playing all eight tiles in one go. Since the board size is the standard 15-by-15, it must be a lot more common to see words stretching across two triple-word-score squares than it is in games where players have only seven tiles at a time!

Greek Scrabble has a very different orthography to English. Though there are Greek letters which look the same as their English counterparts (for example, A, B, K and T), there are several other letters which do not resemble their English equivalents (for example, Δ – delta, Θ – theta, and Λ – lambda). A Greek Scrabble set has 104 tiles, the most common letter being A (alpha), of which there are a dozen tiles.

Russian Scrabble is even less like English than Greek. The Russian set contains 33 different tiles, as well as blanks. Distribution and point values will be totally alien to the English language Scrabble player. There are even more tiles in a Russian set than in a German set, a walloping 126 tiles in all! Russian Scrabble is played with seven tiles at a time on the players' racks.

Spanish Scrabble sets have a round 100 tiles. There is not a K, nor a W. There is a CH tile, worth five points; an LL tile worth eight points; and a Ñ tile and an RR tile, also worth eight points each. The lone Q is worth just five points.

The point values and letter distributions of Dutch, German, Greek, Russian and Spanish Scrabble are shown in the tables here. These details may be of assistance when it comes to tackling the foreign language puzzles.

## DUTCH SCRABBLE:
## THE POINT VALUES AND LETTER DISTRIBUTION

| Letter | Point value | Number of tiles | Letter | Point value | Number of tiles |
|--------|-------------|-----------------|--------|-------------|-----------------|
| A | 1 | 6 | O | 1 | 6 |
| B | 3 | 2 | P | 3 | 2 |
| C | 3 | 2 | Q | 10 | 1 |
| D | 1 | 5 | R | 1 | 6 |
| E | 1 | 18 | S | 1 | 3 |
| F | 5 | 1 | T | 1 | 6 |
| G | 2 | 4 | U | 4 | 2 |
| H | 2 | 3 | V | 4 | 2 |
| I | 1 | 6 | W | 4 | 2 |
| J | 4 | 2 | X | 8 | 1 |
| K | 4 | 2 | Y | 8 | 1 |
| L | 2 | 3 | Z | 6 | 2 |
| M | 3 | 2 | blank | 0 | 2 |
| N | 1 | 10 | | | |

102 tiles in total

## GERMAN SCRABBLE:
## THE POINT VALUES AND LETTER DISTRIBUTION

| Letter | Point value | Number of tiles | Letter | Point value | Number of tiles |
|--------|-------------|-----------------|--------|-------------|-----------------|
| A | 1 | 6 | O | 2 | 4 |
| Ä | 6 | 1 | Ö | 8 | 1 |
| B | 3 | 2 | P | 4 | 1 |
| C | 2 | 4 | Q | 10 | 1 |
| D | 1 | 6 | R | 1 | 7 |
| E | 1 | 16 | S | 1 | 8 |
| F | 3 | 3 | T | 2 | 5 |
| G | 2 | 3 | U | 1 | 6 |
| H | 2 | 5 | Ü | 5 | 1 |
| I | 1 | 9 | V | 4 | 1 |
| J | 6 | 1 | W | 2 | 2 |
| K | 3 | 2 | X | 8 | 1 |
| L | 2 | 4 | Y | 10 | 1 |
| M | 3 | 4 | Z | 3 | 2 |
| N | 1 | 10 | blank | 0 | 2 |

119 tiles in total

131

## GREEK SCRABBLE:
## THE POINT VALUES AND LETTER DISTRIBUTION

| Letter | | Point value | Number of tiles | Letter | | Point value | Number of tiles |
|---|---|---|---|---|---|---|---|
| A | (alpha) | 1 | 12 | Ξ | (xi) | 10 | 1 |
| B | (beta) | 8 | 1 | O | (omicron) | 1 | 9 |
| Γ | (gamma) | 4 | 2 | Π | (pi) | 2 | 4 |
| Δ | (delta) | 4 | 2 | P | (rho) | 2 | 5 |
| E | (epsilon) | 1 | 8 | Σ | (sigma) | 1 | 7 |
| Z | (zeta) | 10 | 1 | T | (tau) | 1 | 8 |
| H | (eta) | 1 | 7 | Y | (upsilon) | 2 | 4 |
| Θ | (theta) | 10 | 1 | Φ | (phi) | 8 | 1 |
| I | (iota) | 1 | 8 | X | (chi) | 8 | 1 |
| K | (kappa) | 2 | 4 | Ψ | (psi) | 10 | 1 |
| Λ | (lambda) | 3 | 3 | Ω | (omega) | 3 | 3 |
| M | (mu) | 3 | 3 | | blank | 0 | 2 |
| N | (nu) | 1 | 6 | | | | |

104 tiles in total

## RUSSIAN SCRABBLE:
## THE POINT VALUES AND LETTER DISTRIBUTION

| Letter | Point value | Number of tiles | Letter | Point value | Number of tiles |
|---|---|---|---|---|---|
| А | 1 | 9 | Р | 1 | 6 |
| Б | 3 | 3 | С | 1 | 5 |
| В | 1 | 5 | Т | 1 | 6 |
| Г | 3 | 3 | У | 2 | 4 |
| Д | 2 | 4 | Ф | 10 | 1 |
| Е | 1 | 10 | Х | 5 | 1 |
| Ё | 3 | 3 | Ц | 5 | 1 |
| Ж | 5 | 2 | Ч | 5 | 1 |
| З | 5 | 2 | Ш | 8 | 1 |
| И | 1 | 10 | Щ | 10 | 1 |
| Й | 4 | 2 | Ъ | 10 | 1 |
| К | 2 | 4 | Ы | 4 | 2 |
| Л | 2 | 4 | Ь | 3 | 2 |
| М | 2 | 4 | Э | 8 | 1 |
| Н | 1 | 6 | Ю | 8 | 1 |
| О | 1 | 11 | Я | 3 | 4 |
| П | 2 | 4 | blank | 0 | 2 |

126 tiles in total

## SPANISH SCRABBLE:
## THE POINT VALUES AND LETTER DISTRIBUTION

| Letter | Point value | Number of tiles | Letter | Point value | Number of tiles |
|--------|-------------|-----------------|--------|-------------|-----------------|
| A | 1 | 12 | Ñ | 8 | 1 |
| B | 3 | 2 | O | 1 | 9 |
| C | 3 | 4 | P | 3 | 2 |
| CH | 5 | 1 | Q | 5 | 1 |
| D | 2 | 5 | R | 1 | 5 |
| E | 1 | 12 | RR | 8 | 1 |
| F | 4 | 1 | S | 1 | 6 |
| G | 2 | 2 | T | 1 | 4 |
| H | 4 | 2 | U | 1 | 5 |
| I | 1 | 6 | V | 4 | 1 |
| J | 8 | 1 | X | 8 | 1 |
| L | 1 | 4 | Y | 4 | 1 |
| LL | 8 | 1 | Z | 10 | 1 |
| M | 3 | 2 | blank | 0 | 2 |
| N | 1 | 5 | | | |

100 tiles in total

# GREEK FOR SCRABBLE

# RUSSIAN FOR SCRABBLE

# FOREIGN SCRABBLE PUZZLES

Here are ten puzzles set in five different foreign languages –
Dutch, German, Greek, Russian and Spanish. Each puzzle
shows a board at a particular stage of a game, as well as the
letters held by one of the players. What is the highest-scoring
move which can be made with the given letters on the relevant
board? You should bear in mind that the point values of the
letters are not necessarily the same as in English Scrabble. The
words used in the puzzles here, and those in the corresponding
solutions, have all been taken from relatively limited
dictionaries of the languages concerned. You won't need the
Greek or Russian equivalents of *The Oxford English Dictionary*
to find the words involved! Crosses are used to indicate blank
tiles. Good luck, especially with the alien characters!

# DUTCH SCRABBLE PUZZLE 1

| | | | | | | | | | | | | | | |
|---|---|---|---|---|---|---|---|---|---|---|---|---|---|---|
| 3W | B | | 2L | | | | 3W | | | | 2L | | | 3W |
| | E | | | | 3L | | | | 3L | | | | 2W | |
| | T | 2W | | | | 2L | | V | | | | 2W | | |
| D | E | P | O | T | | | K | L | O | M | P | | | 2L |
| O | | | | 2W | | | | A | | A | | | | |
| E | 3L | | | | Z | O | E | K | 3L | A | A | R | D | |
| N | O | O | D | R | E | M | | T | | G | | 2L | | |
| 3W | | | E | | | | W | E | I | | Z | I | J | 3W |
| | | 2L | | | | 2L | I | 2L | | | W | 2L | | |
| | 3L | | | | 3L | E | S | | 3L | | I | | 3L | |
| | | | | 2W | E | | S | T | R | I | J | D | | |
| 2L | | G | A | A | R | N | E | | | | N | | | 2L |
| | | U | | | | 2L | L | 2L | | | | 2W | | |
| B | E | L | E | G | E | R | E | N | 3L | | | | 2W | |
| 3W | | | N | | | | N | | | | 2L | | | 3W |

$E_1$ $G_2$ $I_1$ $N_1$ $R_1$ $S_1$ $T_1$

# DUTCH SCRABBLE PUZZLE 2

|   |   |   |   |   |   |   |   |   |   |   |   |   |   |   |
|---|---|---|---|---|---|---|---|---|---|---|---|---|---|---|
| 3W |   |   | 2L |   |   |   | 3W |   |   |   | 2L |   |   | 3W |
|   | 2W |   |   |   | 3L |   |   |   | 3L |   |   |   | 2W |   |
|   |   | 2W |   |   |   | 2L |   | 2L | **P** | **O** | **R** | 2W |   |   |
| 2L |   |   | 2W |   | **S** |   | 2L |   | **R** | 2W |   |   |   | 2L |
| **N** | **E** | **I** | **G** | **I** | **N** | **G** |   |   | **G** |   |   |   |   |   |
|   | 3L |   |   | **A** |   |   |   | 3L | **E** |   |   |   | 3L |   |
|   | 2L |   | **J** | **A** | **A** | **R** | **G** | **E** | **L** | **D** | 2L |   |   |   |
| 3W |   | 2L | **I** | **K** |   | **O** |   |   | **A** | **R** | **E** |   | 3W |   |
|   | **B** |   | **C** |   | 2L | **L** | 2L |   | **M** | 2L |   |   |   |   |
| 3L | **R** |   | **H** | 3L | **M** |   | 3L |   | **H** | **O** | **F** |   |   |   |
| **V** | **E** | **N** | **T** |   | **O** |   |   | **Z** | **E** |   |   |   |   |   |
| 2L | **I** | 2W |   |   | **P** |   |   | **E** | **R** |   |   |   | 2L |   |
|   | **N** |   |   | **O** | **S** | 2L |   | **T** |   | 2W |   |   |   |   |
| 2W |   |   |   | 3L | **U** |   | 3L |   |   |   | 2W |   |   |   |
| 3W |   | 2L |   | **D** | 3W |   |   |   | 2L |   |   |   | 3W |   |

$A_1$  $E_1$  $I_1$  $J_4$  $L_2$  $O_1$  $Z_6$

# GERMAN SCRABBLE PUZZLE 1

|   |   |   |   |   |   |   |   |   |   |   |   |   |   |   |
|---|---|---|---|---|---|---|---|---|---|---|---|---|---|---|
| 3W |   |   | 2L |   |   | 3W |   | **J** |   | 2L |   |   | 3W |
|   | **O** |   |   | **E** | **I** | **N** |   | **O** |   |   | 2W |   |   |
|   | **D** | **A** | **H** | **E** | **R** | 2L |   | **D** |   | 2W |   |   |   |
| 2L | **E** |   | 2W | **I** |   | 2L |   | **E** | **L** | 2W |   |   | 2L |
|   | **R** |   | **N** |   |   |   | 2W | **L** |   |   |   |   |   |
|   | 3L |   | **M** | **I** | **E** | **T** | **E** | **N** |   |   | 3L |   |   |
|   |   | 2L | **A** |   | 2L |   | 2L |   |   | 2L |   |   |   |
| 3W |   | **Q** | **U** | **I** | **T** | **T** |   |   | 2L | **O** | **B** | 3W |
|   | 2L |   | **E** |   | 2L |   | 2L |   |   | **K** |   |   |
|   | 3L |   | **B** | **R** | **A** | **V** |   | 3L |   | **K** | 3L |   |
|   |   | **N** |   | **U** |   |   | 2W |   | **U** |   |   |
| 2L |   | 2W |   | **L** | 2L |   |   | 2W | **L** |   | 2L |
|   | 2W |   | **G** | **E** | **R** | **E** | **I** | **Z** | **T** |   |   |
|   | 2W |   | 3L | **Ä** |   | 3L |   |   | 2W |   |   |
| 3W | **U** | **N** | **T** | **E** | **R** | **W** | **E** | **G** | **S** | 2L | 3W |

| C₃ | E₁ | E₁ | H₂ | N₁ | R₁ | S₁ | U₁ |

137

# GERMAN SCRABBLE PUZZLE 2

|  |  |  |  |  |  |  | J | A |  |  |  |  |  |
|---|---|---|---|---|---|---|---|---|---|---|---|---|---|
|  |  |  |  |  |  |  | U |  |  |  |  |  |  |
|  |  | K | E | G | E | L | N |  | F |  |  |  |  |
|  |  |  | E |  |  |  | G | E | Ü | B | T |  |  |
|  |  |  | R |  |  |  |  |  | R |  |  |  |  |
|  |  |  | L | A | X |  |  |  |  |  |  |  |  |
|  |  |  |  | D |  |  |  |  |  |  |  |  |  |
|  |  |  | B | E | H | U | F | S |  |  |  |  |  |
|  |  |  | E |  |  |  |  | I |  |  |  |  |  |
|  |  |  | W |  |  |  |  | C |  |  |  |  |  |
|  |  | D | Ö | S | E | N |  | H |  |  |  |  |  |
|  |  |  | L |  |  |  |  |  |  |  |  |  |  |
|  |  |  | K |  |  |  |  |  |  |  |  |  |  |
|  | P | U | T | Z | I | G |  |  |  |  |  |  |  |
|  |  |  |  |  |  |  |  |  |  |  |  |  |  |

$A_1$  $F_3$  $H_2$  $M_3$  $R_1$  $T_2$  $U_1$  +

# GREEK SCRABBLE PUZZLE 1

| | | | | | | | | | | | | | | |
|---|---|---|---|---|---|---|---|---|---|---|---|---|---|---|
| 3W | | | 2L | | | 3W | Π | | | 2L | E | | | Π |
| | 2W | | | 3L | | | E | 3L | | E | Y | Γ | | E |
| | | 2W | | | 2L | | Ρ | | | 2W | | | | I |
| 2L | | | 2W | | | Λ | A | Ξ | E | Y | T | O | | Σ |
| | | | 2W | Ψ | | E | | 2W | | | | | | M |
| | 3L | H | T | T | A | M | O | N | O | N | | 3L | | A |
| | 2L | | | Ρ | 2L | O | Y | | | | 2L | | | |
| 3W | | | Θ | E | I | O | N | | | Ω | X | P | A | |
| | 2L | Y | | | 2L | I | 2L | | | P | 2L | | | |
| | 3L | O | Σ | | Λ | A | Δ | E | I | A | | 3L | | |
| Σ | K | N | I | Π | A | | I | | 2W | I | | | | |
| 2L | | A | | B | | 2L | Δ | | | A | | | | 2L |
| | | 2W | | A | 2L | Z | Ω | | | | 2W | | | |
| | 2W | | | 3L | Ω | | | 3L | | | | 2W | | |
| 3W | | 2L | | | H | | | | | 2L | | | | 3W |

A₁  Γ₄  H₁  I₁  Σ₁  T₁  Φ₈

139

# GREEK SCRABBLE PUZZLE 2

| | | | | | | | | | | | | | | |
|---|---|---|---|---|---|---|---|---|---|---|---|---|---|---|
| 3 W | | | 2 L | | | | Δ | | | | 2 L | Ε | | 3 W |
| | 2 W | | | | 3 L | | Ι | | 3 L | | | Τ | 2 W | |
| | | 2 W | | | | 2 L | Α | 2 L | | | | Α | | |
| 2 L | | | 2 W | Ψ | | | Υ | | | Θ | 2 W | Ι | | 2 L |
| | | | | Α | | | Γ | | | Α | Υ | Ρ | Α | |
| | 3 L | | | Ρ | 3 L | | Ε | | 3 L | Μ | | Ο | 3 L | |
| Η | Λ | Ι | Κ | Ι | Α | 2 L | Ι | 2 L | | Ν | | Σ | | |
| 3 W | | | 2 L | | Μ | Ι | Α | Ι | Ν | Ω | 2 L | | | 3 W |
| | | 2 L | | Ν | Α | 2 L | | 2 L | | Δ | | 2 L | | |
| | 3 L | | | Ε | 3 L | | Ξ | | 3 L | Η | | | 3 L | |
| | | | | Φ | Υ | Λ | Ο | Ν | | Σ | Υ | | | |
| 2 L | | | 2 W | Ρ | | | Α | | | | Π | | | 2 L |
| | | 2 W | | Ο | | 2 L | Ν | 2 L | | | Ε | 2 W | | |
| | 2 W | | | Σ | 3 L | | Ο | | 3 L | | Ρ̓ | | 2 W | |
| 3 W | | | 2 L | | | | Ν | | | | 2 L | | | 3 W |

| | | | | | | |
|---|---|---|---|---|---|---|
| Α 1 | Β 8 | Ε 1 | Ζ 10 | Η 1 | Χ 8 | Ω 3 |

# RUSSIAN SCRABBLE PUZZLE 1

# RUSSIAN SCRABBLE PUZZLE 2

ЖЕЛТОК

Я    ПУХ

М    У

К    С

ФАГОТ    Т

А    А    О

К    БТОРОЙ

Е    А

СЪЛЗД    ЧИСЛО

Н    М

И    АР

К    Р

| Б₃ | Д₂ | И₁ | Н₁ | Т₁ | Щ₁₀ | Ь₃ |

# SPANISH SCRABBLE PUZZLE 1

|   |   |   |   |   |   |   |   |   |   | J | U | E | Z |
|---|---|---|---|---|---|---|---|---|---|---|---|---|---|
|   |   |   |   | M | I |   |   |   |   | U |   |   |   |
|   |   |   |   | O |   |   |   |   |   | E |   |   |   |
|   |   |   |   | N |   | LL | E | N | A | R |   |   |   |
|   |   |   |   | T |   |   | E |   |   | G |   |   |   |
|   |   |   |   | A |   |   | V |   |   | A | S | E | O |
|   |   |   |   | Ñ |   |   | A |   |   |   |   |   |   |
| A | C | U | S | A | D | O | R |   |   |   |   |   |   |
|   | O |   |   |   | U |   | S |   |   |   |   |   |   |
|   | C |   |   | Q |   | E |   |   | P | E | N | A |   |
|   | O |   |   | U |   |   | A |   | I |   |   |   |   |
|   |   |   | T | E | S | I | S |   | N |   |   |   |   |
|   |   | M | I |   |   |   | P | I | T | A | R |   |   |
|   |   |   |   |   |   | A | R | A |   |   |   |   |   |
|   |   |   |   |   |   |   |   |   |   |   |   |   |   |

| A₁ | CH₅ | E₁ | I₁ | R₁ | S₁ | T₁ |

143

# SPANISH SCRABBLE PUZZLE 2

Letter tiles:

A₁  C₃  E₁  J₈  O₁  RR₈  U₁

# 9

# SCRABBLE RECORDS

# THE BRITISH NATIONAL SCRABBLE CHAMPIONSHIPS

The British National Scrabble Championship was launched in 1971. Each year sees a variety of regional championships, culminating in the national championship during the summer. The national championship involves 100 players, each of whom has to play three games against randomly chosen opponents. The champion is the person with the highest total score for the three games. Back in 1971, the winning score over the three games was 1,345 points. In the dozen or so years since then, the standard of play has increased considerably, and the champion's score each year seems to go ever higher. Indeed, 1971's winning score of 1,345 points would have only come 24th in the 1983 championship. Even more surprising, 1972's winning score was only 1,215, which would have been only good enough for 55th place in 1983! The champions and their total scores over three games are given here:

| Year | Champion | Total Score |
|------|----------|-------------|
| 1971 | Stephen Haskell | 1,345 |
| 1972 | Olive Behan | 1,215 |
| 1973 | Anne Bradford | 1,266 |
| 1974 | Richard Sharp | 1,288 |
| 1975 | Olive Behan | 1,363 |
| 1976 | Alan Richter | 1,359 |
| 1977 | Michael Goldman | 1,478 |
| 1978 | Philip Nelkon | 1,521 |
| 1979 | Christine Jones | 1,453 |
| 1980 | Joyce Cansfield | 1,540 |
| 1981 | Philip Nelkon | 1,551 |
| 1982 | Russell Byers | 1,626 |
| 1983 | Colin Gumbrell | 1,612 |

How long can the improvement go on?

# THE HIGHEST WINNING MARGIN

Worldwide, the highest winning margin in a real game is believed to be 549 points. This overwhelming victory was achieved by Ron Hendra, of Wimbledon, London, England, during the summer of 1982. His opponent's final score was a rather meagre 180 points. The sets of seven tiles that Ron Hendra had at each turn, and the words that he and his opponent played are given here; so, too, is the final board layout.

Without wishing to detract from Ron Hendra's massive win, it must be noted that his opponent had seven non-scoring turns. Three of the turns involved unallowable words (REW, PILON and WEG); two turns were to exchange tiles; and on two turns, the opponent was unable to play any words at all. All these non-scoring turns certainly assisted Hendra in his record margin.

The dictionary of authority used during this game was the 1972 edition of *Chambers Twentieth Century Dictionary*.

## RON HENDRA

| Move number | Rack | Word(s) played | Score |
|---|---|---|---|
| 1 | AOOOQVZ | ZOA | 24 |
| 2 | MOOOQVY | change | 0 |
| 3 | DEMOOTY | MOOT, ZO | 17 |
| 4 | ADEIITY | OY | 5 |
| 5 | ADEIINT | change | 0 |
| 6 | ADEFINT | DEFIANT, OYE | 84 |
| 7 | IILLORU | LIT | 5 |
| 8 | EGILORU | OUGLIER, RACE | 76 |
| 9 | DEEGOVX | EX, EX, RE | 52 |
| 10 | DEEGNOV | RE, VOE | 8 |
| 11 | DEGINNS | EVOE, SENDING | 81 |
| 12 | ABDFIPS | FAW | 18 |
| 13 | BDEIPSU | BAP, BO | 11 |
| 14 | DEINSTU | DUNITES, REED | 64 |
| 15 | ABIIJK+ | BIKE | 20 |
| 16 | AIJRU++ | FA, JAP | 34 |
| 17 | AIIRU++ | NA | 3 |
| 18 | IIQRU++ | INQUIRE, SOU (using blanks as E and N) | 121 |
| 19 | CDHORSV | DIV | 14 |

## HIS OPPONENT

| Word(s) played | Score |
|---|---|
| EA, TEE, TO | 10 |
| TOT | 4 |
| TEA | 3 |
| CAM | 8 |
| ACE | 6 |
| NAY | 10 |
| REE, TE | 5 |
| TARE, TRACE | 19 |
| HOUR | 24 |
| REW disallowed, WOW | 0 |
| DOW | 14 |
| OW, REE, WE | 21 |
| AS, MA | 14 |
| PILON disallowed | 0 |
| SO | 2 |
| change | 0 |
| change | 0 |
| INQUIRES, LISP | 36 |
| GUN, NA, WEG disallowed | 0 |

| 20 | CHORS | FAH,JO,OH | 51 | NIL,ON | 6 |
| 21 | CRS | UR,UR | 4 | cannot go | 0 |
| 22 | CS | COW,CREE | 14 | cannot go | 0 |
| 23 | S | DOWS,JAPS | 21 | | |
| | | | +2 | | −2 |
| | | Total | 729 | Total | 180 |

| | | | | | | | | | | | | | | |
|---|---|---|---|---|---|---|---|---|---|---|---|---|---|---|
| H | O | U | R | | | | M | A | | 2L | D | | | 3W |
| | U | R | | | 3L | | | S | E | N | D | I | N | G |
| | G | 2W | | | | 2L | | 2L | V | | | V | | |
| 2L | L | | 2W | B | | | 2L | C | O | W | 2W | | | 2L |
| | I | | | I | | | | R | E | E | D | | | |
| | E | | | K | 3L | | T | E | 3L | | U | | | 3L |
| T | R | A | C | E | | T | E | E | | | N | | A | |
| A | | | A | | Z | O | A | | | | I | | I | 3W |
| R | E | 2L | M | O | O | T | | 2L | L | | T | 2L | + | |
| E | X | | | Y | 3L | | N | | I | | E | | Q | |
| | | | D | E | F | I | A | N | T | 2W | S | O | U | |
| 2L | | B | O | | | | Y | | | 2W | | N | I | L |
| | F | A | W | | 2L | | 2L | | | | 2W | | R | |
| J | A | P | S | | 3L | | | 3L | | | | | + | |
| O | H | | 2L | | | 3W | | | | L | I | S | P | |

148

# THE HIGHEST INDIVIDUAL GAME SCORE

The highest score that an individual has achieved in a real game is believed to be 774 points. This heady total was produced by Allan Simmons, of Tottenham, London, England, on 11 July 1981. His opponent's final score was 285 points, giving a winning margin of 489 points. The sets of seven tiles that Allan Simmons had at each turn, and the words he and his opponent played are given here; so, too, is the final board layout.

The dictionary used in this particular game was the 1972 edition of *Chambers Twentieth Century Dictionary*, in which all words used in this game can be found. However, some of the words do not appear in the American Scrabble word bible, *The Official Scrabble Players Dictionary*. They are the following:

| | | ALLAN SIMMONS | | HIS OPPONENT | |
|---|---|---|---|---|---|
| Move number | Rack | Word(s) played | Score | Word(s) played | Score |
| 1 | AEELORU | AUREOLE | 66 | CAR | 11 |
| 2 | EEGINRT | AN, TEERING, UG | 69 | change | 0 |
| 3 | AAFLNOO | change | 0 | change | 0 |
| 4 | AINOPW+ | TO, WO | 15 | TORCH | 20 |
| 5 | AILNPS+ | AUREOLES, SAPLING (using blank as G) | 101 | BIN | 10 |
| 6 | DEENORY | OH, OYE | 17 | AE, BAA, BUG | 19 |
| 7 | DDENORT | DOH | 7 | DOVES, SAPLINGS | 57 |
| 8 | DENORST | DENOTERS disallowed | 0 | EWT, TWO | 24 |
| 9 | DENORST | ERODENTS | 86 | ZEE | 32 |
| 10 | DEIKNRR | DRINKER, ER | 96 | change | 0 |
| 11 | AGIIOTX | AX, EX, KA | 40 | RAJ | 20 |
| 12 | GIIMOTU | IMP | 13 | LEVI disallowed | 0 |
| 13 | EGIMOTU | GJU | 22 | OVA | 7 |
| 14 | EIIMNOT | MEIONITE | 149 | IT, PI, PI | 22 |
| 15 | AHINOQU | IN, MO, QUINOL | 36 | FIT, FY | 22 |
| 16 | AAEFHTT | FA, FY | 21 | LIG, LIMP | 16 |
| 17 | AEHTT | EN, HE, HI | 20 | RAJA (using blank as A) | 10 |
| 18 | ATT | CAST | 12 | OUS, RAJAS | 16 |
| 19 | T | ANT | 3 | | |
| | | | +1 | | −1 |
| | | Total | 774 | Total | 285 |

DOH, ERODENTS, EWT, FY, GJU, LIG, MEIONITE, MO, OUS, OYE, TEERING and UG.
One wonders how much higher Allan Simmons' final score would have been if he hadn't had DENOTERS disallowed and if he had had the second blank. 800 plus certainly looks like it would have been a possibility.

| | | | | | | | | | | | | | | |
|---|---|---|---|---|---|---|---|---|---|---|---|---|---|---|
| 3W | | | 2L | | O | | 3W | | | | 2L | | | 3W |
| | D | | G | | U | | | 3L | | | | | 2W | |
| | R | A | J | + | S | | 2L | | 2L | | | 2W | | |
| H | I | | U | | | | 2L | | | | 2W | | | 2L |
| E | N | | | E | | | | | 2W | | | | | |
| | K | A | | R | 3L | | | | C | | | | 3L | |
| | E | X | | O | V | A | | B | A | A | | 2L | | |
| E | R | | 2L | D | | | A | U | R | E | O | L | E | S |
| W | | T | E | E | R | I | N | G | | | | 2L | | A |
| T | W | O | | N | 3L | | T | | 3L | | L | I | M | P |
| | | R | | T | | | | Q | U | I | N | O | L | |
| 2L | | C | A | S | T | | 2L | | | G | | | | I |
| D | O | H | | | 2L | | 2L | | | | B | I | N | |
| | Y | | | P | I | | | 3L | | | 2W | + | | |
| M | E | I | O | N | I | T | E | | | D | O | V | E | S |

150

# THE HIGHEST SCORE FOR A SINGLE MOVE

The highest score for a single move in a real game is believed to be 392 points. This blockbusting score was managed by Dr Karlo Khoshnaw, of Manchester, England, on 11 April, 1982. He was holding the letters ACEIQSU, and was looking to play the word CAIQUES somewhere on the board. Very fortunately for him, his opponent opened up two triple-word-score squares with a Z between them. Dr Khoshnaw managed to straddle both the triple-word-score squares by playing the word CAZIQUES. The 392 points includes a 50-point bonus.

What does CAZIQUES mean? It is the plural of CAZIQUE – a variant spelling of CACIQUE – which is defined differently by various dictionaries. *Chambers Twentieth Century Dictionary* defines CACIQUE as a West Indian chief or political boss. *The Official Scrabble Players Dictionary* defines CACIQUE as a tropical oriole. *Webster's Third New International Dictionary* gives both these definitions, plus a third one. CACIQUE is also a landowner in the Philippines, according to *Webster's*.

A Scrabble-style board with the following tiles placed:

```
            F
          Y A M
    O   W E D
    I O T A   E
    L   A X E D
        B   H
        O D
      C O U P L E D
        O H
          I
      C A Z I Q U E S
```

# THE HIGHEST SCORE ON THE FIRST MOVE

The highest idealized scores it is possible to achieve on the first move of a game, with from two to seven letters, are given here.

2 letters:  ZO scores 22 points. A ZO is one of a kind of hybrid domestic cattle from the Himalayas.

3 letters:  ZAX scores 38 points. A ZAX is a chopper for trimming slates. ZAX occurs in a variety of English dictionaries. The same cannot be said for another three-letter word which also scores 38 points. The word is ZIJ, defined by *Funk and Wagnall's* as the Persian astronomical tables, revised and corrected by Omar Khayyam. Rather surprisingly, ZIJ does not begin with a capital letter.

4 letters:  QUIZ scores 48 points, and can be found in just about every dictionary.

5 letters:  SQUIZ, a glance or look, scores 66 points. Other high-scoring five-letter words are JAZZY, QUAKY, ZANJA, ZINKY, ZIPPY and ZYMIC, all of which score 62 points.

6 letters:  QUEAZY, causing nausea, scores 74 points.

7 letters:  QYRGHYZ scores 140 points. This word is given in *Webster's Third New International Dictionary* as a variant spelling of KIRGHIZ, a widespread people of central Asia. According to *Webster's*, QYRGHYZ is usually capitalized. If this can be interpreted as meaning that QYRGHYZ is sometimes *not* capitalized, then QYRGHYZ is a fine Scrabble word! On the other hand, *Webster's Third New International* invariably labels all proper nouns as 'usually capitalized'. So perhaps Scrabble players should treat QYRGHYZ as a proper noun, and hence as an invalid word. Second only to QYRGHYZ is ZYXOMMA, a type of Indian dragonfly, found in *Funk and Wagnall's*. This scores 130 points, and is also notable for having its letters in reverse alphabetical order! Other high-scoring seven-letter words are QUARTZY and SQUEEZY.

# THE HIGHEST SCORE ON THE FIRST TWO MOVES

The highest idealized score it is possible to achieve on the first two moves of a game is 365 points.

The first player puts down XICAQUE for 120 points, with the X on the centre square. The second player plays MUZJIKS perpendicular to XICAQUE, making XICAQUES. This move scores 245 points, giving a total of 365 points for the two moves.

XICAQUES, MUZJIKS? What do these strange-looking words mean? XICAQUE is a variant spelling of JICAQUE, an Indian people of northern Honduras, so XICAQUES are individual members of these people. MUZJIKS is the plural of MUZJIK, a Russian peasant. Both words are in *Webster's Third New International Dictionary*.

MUZJIK

XICAQUES

# THE HIGHEST SCORE ON THE FIRST THREE MOVES

The highest idealized score it is possible to achieve with the first three moves of a game is 664 points.

This incredible three-move total is achieved as follows. The first player puts down ANALYZE with the Z falling on the double-letter-score square. This is worth 108 points. The second player follows with REQUIEM and ANALYZER, notching up 146 points. Then the first player makes PSYCHOANALYZERS for a whopping 410 points. Hence a grand total of 664 points.

Three of these four words are in *The Official Scrabble Players Dictionary* – ANALYZE, ANALYZER and REQUIEM. To find PSYCHOANALYZER as a noun, turn to *Webster's New International Dictionary* (Second edition).

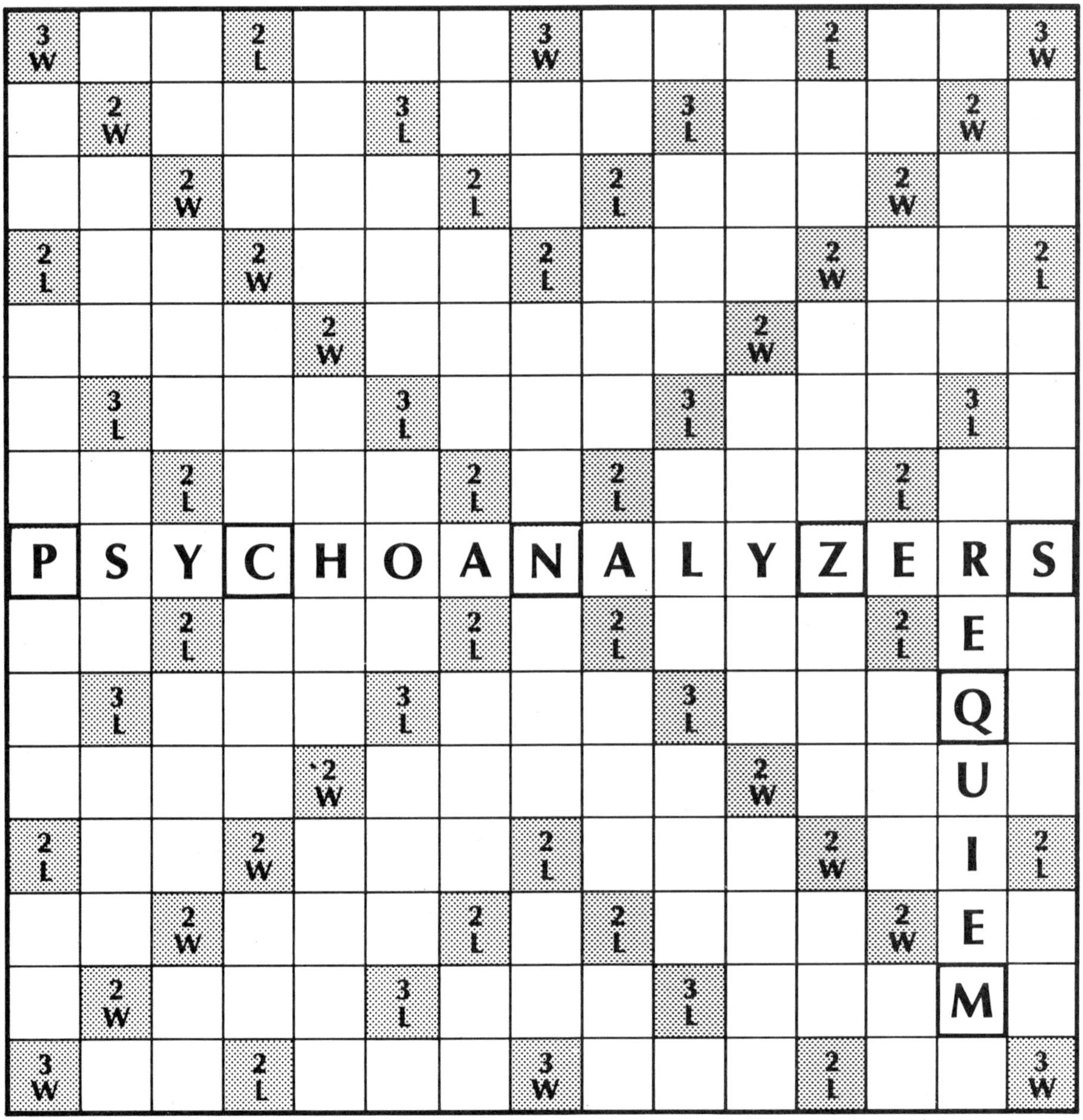
PSYCHOANALYZERS
REQUIEM

# THE HIGHEST SCORE ON THE FIRST FOUR MOVES

The highest idealized score known to be achievable on the first four moves of a game is 857 points.

Player one begins with the word CHARQUI, and scores 112 points. Note that the Q falls on the double-letter-score square. The second player follows this with PHYSICAL for a mere 72 points. The first player now turns PHYSICAL into DEPHYSICALIZING, which stretches across two triple-word-score squares, and scores 464 points. The second player then follows with JACKSAW and CHARQUIS.

CHARQUI, CHARQUIS and PHYSICAL are all given in *The Official Scrabble Players Dictionary*. JACKSAW and DEPHYSICALIZING are both in *Webster's New International Dictionary* (Second edition).

DEPHYSICALIZING

CHARQUI (reading down from C in DEPHYSICALIZING)

JACKSAW

# THE HIGHEST SCORE IN THE FIRST FIVE MOVES

The highest idealized score which can be made on the first five moves of a game is a staggering 1,610, almost twice as many points as the highest score achievable on the first four moves.

The first player begins with LOCKING for 84 points. The second player follows with FLEXUOSE, for 118 points. Back to the first player, who puts down HYDRO and OF for just 21 points. The second player then responds with REE, RE, EX and EU for even fewer points, a mere 16. Then the first player comes back with a bang and makes DEHYDROFREEZING, FLOCKING, ZO, IS and NE, scoring 1,371 points. The total for these five moves is 1,610 points.

With just three exceptions, these words are in *The Official Scrabble Players Dictionary*. The exceptions are: DEHYDROFREEZING, which is in some addenda sections of *Webster's New International Dictionary* (Second edition); EU comes·from the same dictionary, and is an adjective meaning good, well, true, or typical; and ZO is in both the 1972 and 1983 editions of *Chambers Twentieth Century Dictionary*.

# DEHYDROFREEZING

Across (row 2): FLEXUOSE

Down (column starting at F): FLOCKING

# THE HIGHEST SCORE IN THE FIRST SIX MOVES

The highest idealized score for the first six moves of a game is 1,768 points. The set-up required for this is the same as for the first five moves, followed by either BUCKJUMP or JACKSHAY across the K of FLOCKING. This scores an additional 158 points, for a grand total of 1,768 points.

# HIGHER STILL?

The highest scores for two moves, three moves, four moves, five moves and six moves were all devised by Kyle Corbin, of Raleigh, North Carolina, USA, and appeared in the November 1982 edition of *Word Ways*, The Journal of Recreational Linguistics.

Can you better any of Kyle's highest scores? Can you go on to find the highest scores achievable with seven moves, eight moves, and so on?

DEHYDROFREEZING

FLEXUOSE

FLOCKING

BUCKJUMP

# N-TILE RECORDS

What is the highest score achievable by playing a given number of tiles at a single turn of Scrabble? In other words, what is the highest score possible for playing just one tile? And what about two tiles? And three, four, five, six and seven tiles?

The answers to all these questions are again provided by Kyle Corbin, whose findings were published in the May 1983 edition of *Word Ways*, The Journal of Recreational Linguistics, and are summarized here. Of course, it may be possible to improve on Kyle Corbin's scores. If you can manage to do so, please send your solutions to the publisher.

# THE 1-TILE RECORD

Just by playing a solitary S, it is possible to score as many as 231 points, using the words HYDROXYBENZENES and QUICKSILVERINGS. Make the following moves, until you arrive at the board layout shown here.

1. SNOW
2. SNOWBALL
3. SILVER
4. SILVERING
5. QUICKSILVERING
6. ERG
7. BENZENE, EN, RE
8. HYDROXYBENZENE

And then play the solitary S:

9. HYDROXYBENZENES, QUICKSILVERINGS

This last move notches up 231 points.

All of the words played can be found in *Webster's Third New International Dictionary*.

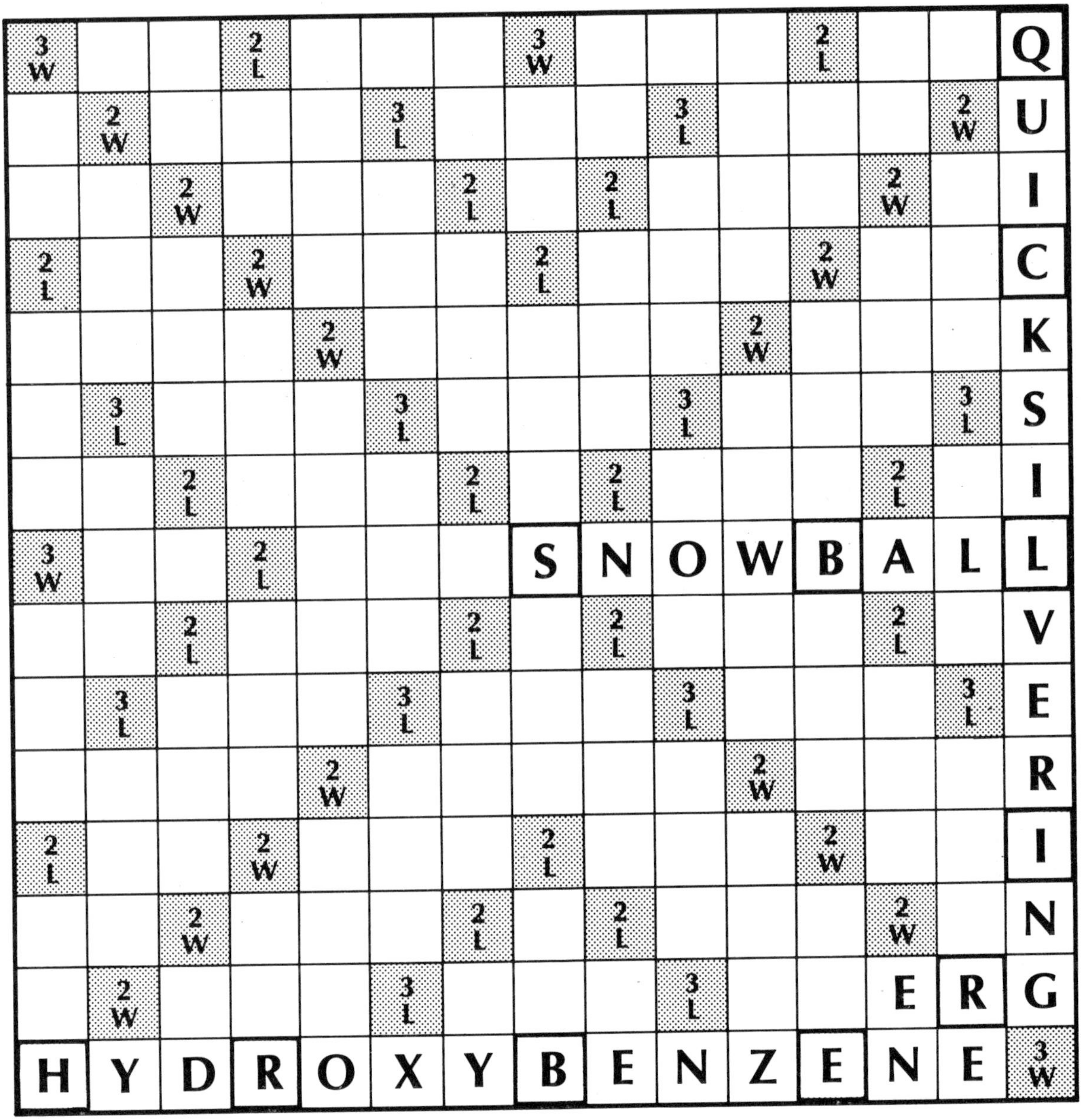
QUICKSILVERING
SNOWBALL
ERG
HYDROXYBENZENE

# THE 2-TILE RECORD

Kyle Corbin's top score for playing just two tiles is 498 points. To reach these dizzy heights, Kyle makes use of three long words, two of which cross triple-word-score squares, and one of which crosses two triple-word-score squares. The ten moves leading up to the board layout needed for this record-breaking score are as follows:

1. DRAM
2. DRAMATIC
3. SUBJECT
4. SUBJECTIVIZE
5. BE, BE
6. PHYLLITE
7. ANTHOPHYLLITE
8. UP, PA
9. EAU
10. MACQUEREAU

Then, on the 11th move play an X and an S, thus:

11. XANTHOPHYLLITES, MACQUEREAUX, SUBJECTIVIZES

That one move alone, just using two tiles, is worth an amazing 498 points.

All words are in *Webster's Third New International Dictionary*.

MACQUEREAU

PANTHOPHYLLITE

DRAMATI

SUBJECTIVIZE

# THE 3-TILE RECORD

According to Kyle, searching for the three-tile record was certainly the most challenging and intriguing of the various n-tile problems. Would it be possible to play each of the three tiles on a triple-word-score square, forming a triple-triple-triple 15-letter word? Such a word would have to become two six-letter words when its first, eighth and last letters were removed. There are very few such words. The only ones known are:

PRECOMBINATIONS (giving RECOMB and NATION)
TROUBLESHOOTERS (giving ROUBLE and HOOTER)
SNIPPERSNAPPERS (giving NIPPER and NAPPER)
WHIPPERSNAPPERS (giving HIPPER and NAPPER)
SCRATCHBRUSHERS (giving CRATCH and RUSHER)

It was the last of these that Kyle used in his three-tile record. The 13 moves leading up to the board layout just prior to the record move are:

1. KILO
2. KILOWATT
3. QUADRAT
4. QUADRATOJUGAL (the J is a blank)
5. EL, ER
6. RUSHER
7. SUE, ER
8. ZEBU
9. CRATCH, SH
10. TIC
11. UM, UT, TI
12. PTERYGIUM
13. MYXOPTERYGIUM

And then, on the 14th move, play three tiles, S, B and S, thus:

14. SCRATCHBRUSHERS, MYXOPTERYGIUMS, ZEBUB, QUADRATOJUGALS

Just to repeat the total score for that last move: 978 points! As with the one- and two-tile records, all words can be found in *Webster's Third New International Dictionary*.

Scrabble-style board grid (premium squares: 3W = triple word, 2W = double word, 3L = triple letter, 2L = double letter):

| | | | | | | | | | | | | | | |
|---|---|---|---|---|---|---|---|---|---|---|---|---|---|---|
| 3W | M | Y | X | O | P | T | E | R | Y | G | I | U | M | 3W |
| | 2W | | | | 3L | | | | 3L | | | T | I | C |
| | | 2W | | | 2L | | 2L | | | | 2W | | | R |
| 2L | | | 2W | | | | 2L | | | | 2W | | | A |
| | | | | 2W | | | | | 2W | | | | | T |
| | 3L | | | | 3L | | | 3L | | | | | 3L | C |
| | | 2L | | | | K | | Z | E | B | U | | S | H |
| 3W | | | 2L | | | I | | | | | | | E | 3W |
| | | 2L | | | | L | | 2L | | | | 2L | | R |
| | 3L | | | | 3L | O | | | 2W | | | | 3L | U |
| 2L | | | 2W | | | W | | | | | 2W | | | S |
| | | 2W | | | 2L | A | 2L | | | | 2W | | | H |
| | 3L | | | | 3L | T | | 3L | | | | | E | E |
| | 2W | | | | 3L | T | | | 3L | | | | | R |
| 3W | Q | U | A | D | R | A | T | O | + | U | G | A | L | 3W |

169

# THE 4-TILE RECORD

Onwards and upwards! With just four tiles, it is possible to score well over 1,000 points in just one move. Kyle Corbin's record here is 1,247 points. Fifteen moves are required to achieve the board layout just prior to the blockbusting move. The moves are:

1. STROP
2. PREENING
3. PREJUDGE
4. BID
5. WADE
6. CLAUSTROPHOBIA (the H is a blank)
7. RAGES
8. QUADRAGESIMA
9. WA, WY
10. BONY
11. DA
12. ETHOXY, WY
13. ID, DE
14. NAZI
15. ASHKENAZI

Then on the 16th move, play the four tiles M, C, R and L:

16. METHOXYCARBONYL, ASHKENAZIM, CLAUSTROPHOBIAC, PREJUDGER, QUADRAGESIMAL

Again, the score for that last move is 1,247 points!

*Webster's Third New International Dictionary* is still the authority for all the words played here.

ASHKENAZI

CLAUSTROP+OBIA

PREJUDGE

QUADRAGESIMA

DETHOXY

171

# THE 5-TILE RECORD

With five tiles, it is possible to score 1,497 points. Not surprisingly, the board layout is more complicated and it takes 21 moves to reach the arrangement of words needed to achieve the 1,497 points. Those 21 moves are:

1. UP
2. RIGHTFUL
3. ORE
4. HYDRO, OO
5. REE, RE
6. TJANTING
7. NAVVIED (the second V is a blank)
8. ULVA
9. MAJAGUAS
10. AM, AMA (the M is a blank)
11. AT, TAM
12. OGIVE, TAMIL, EA
13. OVERS, VULVA, EA, RS
14. EXTROVERSIONS, EM, XAT, RAMA
15. TEE
16. EQUINE
17. IN, IE
18. EDEN
19. NOMIC
20. ASTRONOMIC
21. ASTRONOMICALLY

Then on the 22nd move, the five tiles D, E, F, Z and G are played:

22. DEHYDROFREEZING, DEXTROVERSIONS, EMAJAGUAS, FRIGHTFUL, ZEQUINE, GASTRONOMICALLY

Not bad, 1,497 points for just a handful of tiles!

All words are from *Webster's Third New International Dictionary*.

EXTROVERSIONS

MAJAGUAS

H · TA+IL
Y · NAV+IED · TEA
D · T
R · I
O · O · N

RIGHTFUL
RE · P
E
ET

EQUINE
IE · D
N · E

ASTRONOMICALLY

# THE 6-TILE RECORD

With six tiles, a score of 1,729 points is possible. Just follow the first 25 moves outlined below, and then gasp in amazement at the last move!

1. WORKS
2. RUSHWORKS
3. ADDER
4. FORMAT
5. FORMATIVE
6. REFORMATIVE
7. ERG
8. ERG
9. HEN
10. EAR
11. PACIFIC, PEAR
12. CALF
13. FEAR
14. ENATES, AN, IT, IS
15. YA
16. SWING
17. OOGAMETE
18. ALMUDE
19. JINGLE, JO, IO, GA, EE
20. TI, IJO
21. LOQUENT
22. LOQUENTLY
23. NE, EL
24. ON
25. UTA, AJINGLE

And then play the six tiles O, X, P, B, Z and E:

26. OXYPHENBUTAZONE, OPACIFICATIONS, XENATES, PREFORMATIVE, BRUSHWORKS, ZOOGAMETE, ELOQUENTLY

If you can improve on 1,729 points in just six tiles, please pass your solution on to the publisher.

All words are courtesy of *Webster's Third New International Dictionary*.

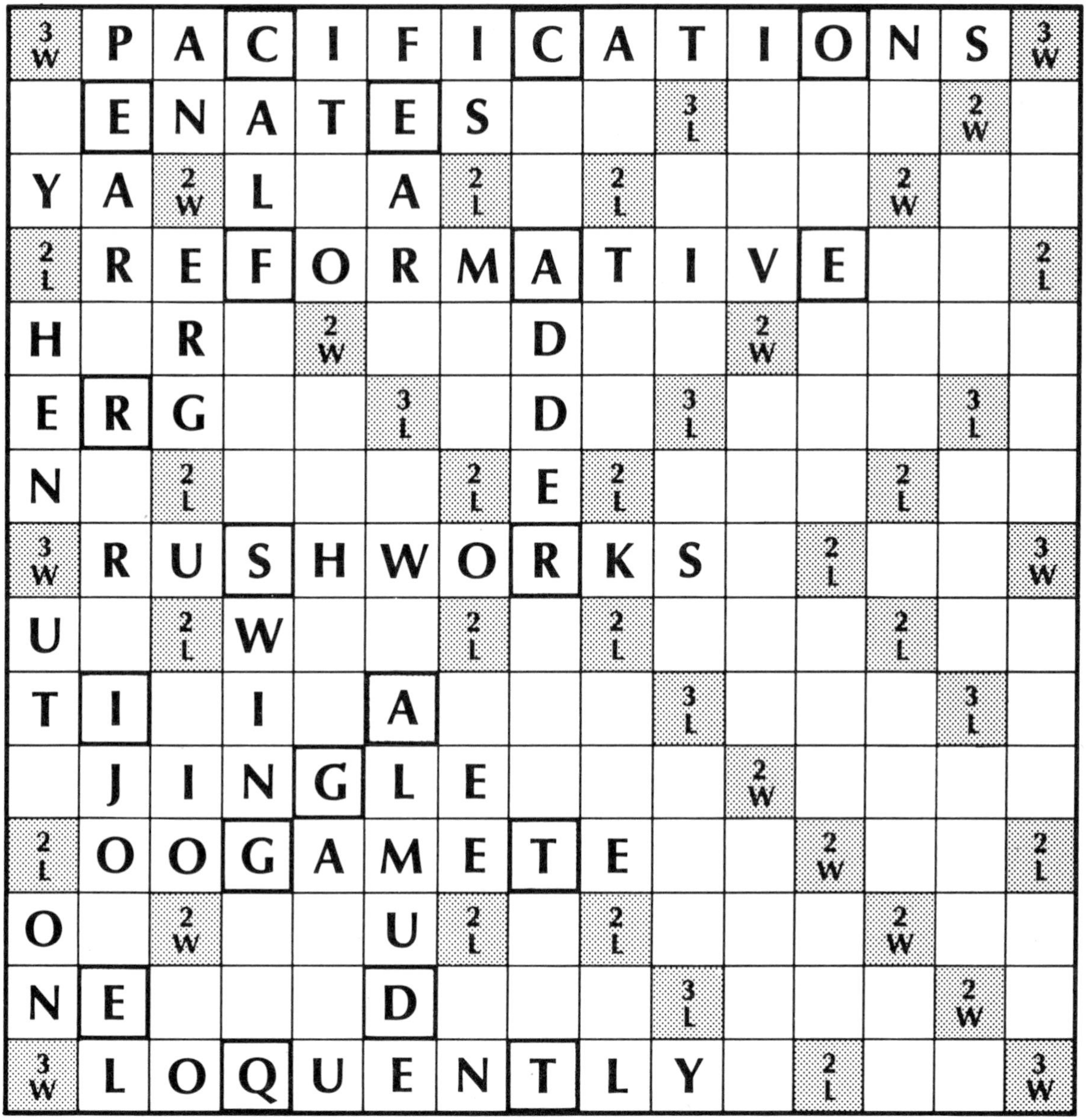

Scrabble-style crossword grid (15×15 board):

- Row 1: **P A C I F I C A T I O N S** (corners: 3W)
- Row 2: **E N A T E S** (3L, 2W)
- Row 3: **Y A** (2W) **L** (2L) **A** (2L) (2W)
- Row 4: **R E F O R M A T I V E** (2L left, 2L right)
- Row 5: **H** / **R** / **R** (2W) **D** (2W)
- Row 6: **E** / **R G** (3L) **D** (3L) (3L right)
- Row 7: **N** (2L) (2L) **E** (2L) (2L)
- Row 8: **R U S H W O R K S** (3W left, 2L, 3W right)
- Row 9: **U** / **I** (2L) **W** (2L) **A** (2L) (2L)
- Row 10: **T I** / **I** / **A** (3L) (3L)
- Row 11: **J I N G L E** (2W)
- Row 12: **O O G A M E T E** (2L, 2W, 2L)
- Row 13: **O** / **U** (2L) (2L) (2W)
- Row 14: **N E** / **D** (3L) (2W)
- Row 15: **L O Q U E N T L Y** (3W corners, 2L)

# THE 7-TILE RECORD

Kyle Corbin's record for playing seven tiles is 1,794 points. The board layout and the words made are almost identical to his six-tile record. The first 24 moves are exactly the same as for the six-tile record, and the 25th move becomes the blockbuster, with the word AJINGLE being played at the same time as the other high-scoring words. Thus, move 25 involves the letters O, X, P, B, A, Z and E:

25. OXYPHENBUTAZONE, OPACIFICATIONS, XENATES, PREFORMATIVE, BRUSHWORKS, AJINGLE, ZOOGAMETE, ELOQUENTLY

Playing AJINGLE adds an extra 15 points to the six-tile record, but a further 50 points must also be added, that being the bonus score for using all seven tiles in one go.
The final score, then, for playing all seven tiles is 1,794.

Again, all words can be found in *Webster's Third New International Dictionary*.

PACIFICATIONS
ENATES
REFORMATIVE
RUSHWORKS
AJINGLE
OOGAMETE
LOQUENTLY

# BEYOND WEBSTER'S

Does Kyle Corbin's seven-tile record of 1,794 points represent the ultimate in Scrabble? Is there any way in which a higher score can be achieved in just one turn? Yes, there is!

The record scores managed by Corbin for two, three, four, five, six and seven tiles all involved words from just one dictionary – *Webster's Third New International Dictionary*. By making use of words in other authoritative sources, the seven-tile record score of 1,794 points can be considerably improved.

The all-time record currently stands at 1,962 points. This solution was devised by Jeff Grant, of Hastings, New Zealand, and it originally appeared in the May 1979 edition of *Word Ways*, a journal of word games and word puzzles which has been referred to several times already. Grant's 1,962-point solution was based on a 1,961-point solution devised by Darryl Francis, of Surrey, England, and Ron Jerome, of Bracknell, Berkshire, England. This 1,961-point solution appeared in the May 1974 edition of *Word Ways*.

Jeff Grant's 1,962-pointer requires 28 moves to get the board layout ready for his top-scoring solution to be added. Here are those 28 moves:

1. ER
2. SQUANDER
3. ODD
4. OOT
5. DU, TUE
6. TRI, DUT
7. SQUANDERMANIA
8. IM, FA, UN, LI, LA, DUTIFULL
9. ELAT
10. EX, OX
11. AMP, TA
12. GOYIM (the Y is a blank)
13. GAUDE
14. IE
15. IN, EN
16. ODEA (the D is a blank)
17. PROVER
18. AITTS
19. EEVN, ES
20. VAGABOND
21. VAGABONDAGE

22. WIN
23. LEEDS, WE, IE
24. FLOWERET
25. TIEW
26. IO
27. RICKSHAW, AR, BI, OC, WINK, AH, GA
28. JINNYRICKSHAW, AN, GY

The 29th move uses the seven letters B, Z, Y, C, H, R and S:

29. BENZOXYCAMPHORS, PROVERB, GAUDEZ,
    DUTIFULLY, SQUANDERMANIAC, FLOWERETH,
    VAGABONDAGER, JINNYRICKSHAWS

The words used here come from a variety of dictionaries; no one
dictionary contains all 56 of the words involved. Brief
definitions of the words, and an indication of one or two
dictionaries that list the words, are given below.

| Word | Definition | Dictionary |
|---|---|---|
| AH | an interjection | Ch83, OSPD |
| AITTS | oats | OED |
| AMP | ampere | Ch83, OSPD |
| AN | the indefinite article | Ch83, OSPD |
| AR | the letter R | Ch83, OSPD |
| BENZOXYCAMPHORS | plural of 'benzoxycamphor', a chemical compound of camphor and the benzoxy radical | W2 |
| BI | a person attracted to both sexes | OSPD |
| DU | a variant of 'do' | W3 |
| DUT | an obsolete form of 'doubt' | OED |
| DUTIFULL | an early form of 'dutiful' | OED |
| DUTIFULLY | in a dutiful manner | Ch 83, W3 |
| EEVN | an old spelling of 'even' | Ch83, OED |
| ELAT | an obsolete form of 'elate' | OED |
| EN | the letter N | Ch83, OSPD |
| ER | an interjection | Ch83, OSPD |
| ES | the letter S | Ch83, OSPD |
| EX | the letter X | Ch83, OSPD |
| FA | a musical tone | Ch83, OSPD |
| FLOWERET | a small flower | Ch83, OSPD |
| FLOWERETH | the archaic third person singular present indicative of the verb 'flower' | OED |
| GA | a people of Ghana | W3 |
| | a Scots variant of 'gall' | W2 |
| | an obsolete form of 'go' | OED |
| GAUDE | a rosary bead | OED |

| Word | Definition | Dictionary |
|---|---|---|
| GAUDEZ | prayers beginning with the word 'gaude' | OED |
| GOYIM | the plural of 'goy', a non-Jewish person | Ch83, OSPD |
| GY | a Scots variant of 'guy' | OED |
| IE | a Pacific Islands screw pine | W2, W3 |
| IM | an obsolete form of 'him' | OED |
| IN | a preposition | Ch83, OSPD |
| IO | an interjection | Ch83, W3 |
| JINNYRICKSHAW | a rickshaw | OED |
| JINNYRICKSHAWS | the plural of 'jinnyrickshaw' | OED |
| LA | a musical tone | Ch83, OSPD |
| LEEDS | manners of speaking | OED, W3 |
| LI | a Chinese unit of distance | Ch83, OSPD |
| OC | { an old past tense of the verb 'ache' { yes | OED |
| ODD | unusual | W2 |
| ODEA | concert halls | Ch83, OSPD |
| OOT | out | Ch83, OSPD |
| OX | an animal | OSPD, W3 |
| PROVER | one that proves | Ch83, OSPD |
| PROVERB | a saying | Ch83, OSPD |
| RICKSHAW | a passenger vehicle | Ch83, OSPD |
| SQUANDER | to spend wastefully | Ch83, OSPD |
| SQUANDERMANIA | spirit of reckless expenditure | Ch83, OSPD |
| SQUANDERMANIAC | a squanderer | Ch83, W3 |
| TA | an expression of gratitude | W2 |
| TIEW | fishing tackle | Ch83, OSPD |
| TRI | a black, tan and white dog | OED |
| TUE | the nozzle of a smith's bellows | W3 |
| UN | one | OED |
| VAGABOND | a vagrant | Ch83, OSPD |
| VAGABONDAGE | vagrancy | Ch83, OSPD |
| VAGABONDAGER | a vagrant | Ch83, W3 |
| WE | a pronoun | OED, W2 |
| WIN | to be victorious | Ch83, OSPD |
| WINK | to close and open an eye quickly | Ch83, OSPD |
| | | Ch83, OSPD |

(The abbreviations for the dictionaries are: Ch83 – *Chambers Twentieth Century Dictionary* (1983 edition); OED – *The Oxford English Dictionary*; OSPD – *The Official Scrabble Players Dictionary*; W2 – *Webster's New International Dictionary* (Second edition); and W3 – *Webster's Third New International Dictionary*. Fuller details of all these sources can be found in the Bibliography.)

Scrabble-style puzzle grid (premium squares: 3W = triple word, 2W = double word, 3L = triple letter, 2L = double letter; "+" = blank tile):

| 1 | 2 | 3 | 4 | 5 | 6 | 7 | 8 | 9 | 10 | 11 | 12 | 13 | 14 | 15 |
|---|---|---|---|---|---|---|---|---|----|----|----|----|----|----|
| 3W |  |  | 2L |  |  |  | 3W |  |  |  | 2L |  |  | 3W |
|  | 2W |  |  |  | 3L |  | S |  | 3L |  |  |  | 2W | J |
|  |  | 2W |  |  |  | 2L | Q | 2L |  |  |  | 2W |  | I |
| 2L |  |  | 2W |  |  |  | U |  |  |  | E | E | V | N |
|  |  |  |  | 2W |  |  | A | I | T | T | S |  | A | N |
|  | 3L |  |  |  | 3L | O | N |  | 3L |  |  |  | G | Y |
|  |  | 2L |  |  |  | O | D | D |  | F |  | 2L | A | R |
| P |  |  | 2L |  | T | U | E |  |  | L |  |  | B | I |
| R |  | 2L |  |  |  | T | R | I |  | O |  | 2L | O | C |
|  | 3L |  |  | G | O | + | I | M | 3L |  | W | I | N | K |
| O | + | E | A | 2W | F | A |  |  |  | L | E | E | D | S |
| V |  | U | 2W |  | U | N | 2L |  |  | R |  |  | A | H |
| E |  | D |  |  | L | I |  | 2L |  | E |  | 2W | G | A |
| R | I | E |  | E | L | A | T | T | 3L | T | I | E | E | W |
| 3W | E | N | 2L | O | X |  | 3W | A | M | P | 2L | O |  | 3W |

# BEYOND 1,962 POINTS . . .

Just running your eye down the list of words used in the creation of the 1,962-point move gives an idea of the difficulty involved in record attempts at this very rarefied level. Is it possible to go beyond 1,962 points? Yes, quite likely, but no one has come up with such a solution yet. If there is such a solution, it will undoubtedly involve a fair sprinkling of obsolete words dredged up from *The Oxford English Dictionary*.

The key to improving on 1,962 points probably lies in finding a better word than BENZOXYCAMPHORS. That word alone contributes 1,593 points to the total score; that is, $59 \times 3 \times 3 \times 3$. Are there any words which score more than 59, before they are tripled, tripled, and tripled again? A candidate which has been suggested is the non-dictionary word SESQUIOXIDIZING. This is worth 62 points, and so if it could be worked into a high-scoring solution would contribute $62 \times 3 \times 3 \times 3$ (or 1,674) points to the total, quite an improvement on BENZOXYCAMPHORS.

But what is SESQUIOXIDIZING? If it isn't in a dictionary, how can its candidacy be justified?

*Webster's Third New International Dictionary* includes three words which are relevant to the discussion. They are:

OXIDE – a compound of oxygen with an element

OXIDIZE – to combine with oxygen (the -ED, -ING and -S forms being indicated)

SESQUIOXIDE – an oxide containing three atoms of oxygen combined with two of the other constituent in the molecule (for example, $Fe_2O_3$ is iron sesquioxide)

*The Oxford English Dictionary* includes a couple more words that should be noted:

SESQUIOXIDATION – conversion into a sesquioxide

SESQUIOXIDIZED – converted into a sesquioxide

But the *Oxford* does *not* give the infinitive form SESQUIOXIDIZE nor the present participle, SESQUIOXIDIZING. Which makes life tough for the Scrabble-playing record-breaker!

An enquiry to the publishers of the *Webster* dictionaries, G. and C. Merriam, did elicit the fact that the verb SESQUIOXIDIZE *does* appear in their files. The word was considered during the early 1930s for possible inclusion in the Second Edition of their *New International Dictionary*, published in 1934, but it had too few citations. Accordingly, the editors of the Second Edition passed it over.

So, you see, SESQUIOXIDIZE does exist, albeit not in any dictionary. And this implies that the present participle SESQUIOXIDIZING can be formed, but that's not in any dictionary either. Which is pretty frustrating!

Even so, can you devise a Scrabble move using the word SESQUIOXIDIZING and which scores more than 1,962 points? Is 2,000 plus a possibility?

# THE ULTIMATE SCORE FOR A SINGLE MOVE

Suppose that *any* combination of letters counts as a valid Scrabble word. In this version of the game, Scrabble is reduced to a purely mathematical exercise, one in which players alternately place one to seven numbered tiles on the board in such a fashion as to maximize their own score and minimize their opponent's opportunities.

In this totally mathematical game of Scrabble, what is the highest score that can be made on just one move? The answer: 3,119 points! This represents the ultimate score achievable with just seven tiles. It is interesting to note that the record score of 1,962 points using *real* words is not quite two-thirds of this ultimate score.

To obtain this 3,119-point score, all attention must be directed to forming a single fifteen-letter 'word' across the top of the Scrabble board containing all letters with values of 5 or more. The Q and the Z must be played on positions 4 and 12, and J, X and K must be played on positions 1, 8 and 15; F, H, V, W and Y can be distributed in any order among the remaining positions. However, there is considerable latitude in the arrangement of the other 84 letters. Obviously, any letter can be swapped with one of equivalent value. Less obviously, the letters B, C, D, G, M and P can be arranged in any way whatever in the columns headed by J, K and X. Furthermore, the letters I, L, R, S, T and U can be assigned to any column headed by F, Q and Z. The seven tiles J, F, F, Q, K, Z and X are played on the final move of this game, and score 3,119 points!

The idea of mathematical Scrabble originated with Dr Ralph Beaman, of Boothwyn, Pennsylvania, USA. His 3,119-point move appeared in the November 1974 edition of *Word Ways*.

| J | F | F | Q | H | H | V | K | V | W | W | Z | Y | Y | X |
|---|---|---|---|---|---|---|---|---|---|---|---|---|---|---|
| B | O | O | O | O | 3L | O | C | O | 3L | O | O | U | + | P |
| B | I | I | I |   | 2L |   | C | 2L |   |   |   | 2W |   | P |
| G | I | I | I |   |   |   | M |   |   |   | 2W |   |   | D |
| G | I | I | I | 2W |   |   | M |   | 2W |   |   |   |   | D |
| G | L | L | L |   | 3L |   | D |   | 3L |   |   |   | 3L | D |
| A | R | R | R |   |   | 2L | A | 2L |   |   |   | 2L |   | A |
| A | R | R | R |   |   |   | A |   |   | 2L |   |   |   | A |
| E | T | T | T |   |   | 2L | E | 2L |   |   |   | 2L |   | E |
| A | S | S | S |   | 3L |   | A |   | 3L |   |   |   | 3L | A |
| E | T | T | T | 2W |   |   | E |   | 2W |   |   |   |   | E |
| E | U | U | U |   |   |   | E |   |   | 2W |   |   |   | E |
| E | L | S |   |   | 2L |   | E | 2L |   |   |   | 2W |   | E |
| N | 2W |   |   | 3L |   |   | N |   | 3L |   |   |   | 2W | N |
| N |   |   | 2L |   |   |   | N |   |   |   | 2L |   |   | N |

# THE ULTIMATE SCORE FOR A COMPLETE GAME

Still sticking with Ralph Beaman's idea of mathematical Scrabble, what is the highest complete game score (for both players)? Again, *any* combination of letters is counted as a valid 'word'.

Ralph Beaman offered a 5,609-point total in *Word Ways* in November 1974. This was subsequently boosted to 5,874 points by Stephen Root, of Westboro, Massachusetts, USA; and this, in turn, was bettered by Charles Brown, of Albuquerque, New Mexico, USA. Charles Brown's record game score of 5,876 points was published in the February 1983 edition of *Word Ways*.

There are 44 moves in this record-breaking game, and they are given here, along with the score made at each move:

| Move number | 'Word(s)' played | Score |
|---|---|---|
| 1. | AAAAAAA | 66 |
| 2. | EEEEEEE, AAAAAAAE | 67 |
| 3. | FV, EV | 13 |
| 4. | HH, EH, EH | 18 |
| 5. | HHV, EV | 17 |
| 6. | WW, EW | 13 |
| 7. | WWY | 12 |
| 8. | IIEEEEEEEIIIII, IF, IW, IY | 136 |
| 9. | FFVQHHVKWWYZYDD, IF, EQ, AAAAAAEK, IZ, IY, ID | 2,557 |
| 10. | INNANNAN, IEH, NEH, NEV, NEW, NIW, AIY, NIZ | 110 |
| 11. | TINNANNAN, TEQ | 21 |
| 12. | ITINNANNANN, IEV, NIY | 68 |
| 13. | ETEQ | 26 |
| 14. | TETEQ | 14 |
| 15. | ETETEQ | 15 |
| 16. | TETETEQ | 16 |
| 17. | ETETETEQ | 18 |
| 18. | TETETETEQ | 18 |
| 19. | ETETETETEQ | 19 |
| 20. | TETETETETEQ | 20 |
| 21. | ETETETETETEQ | 42 |
| 22. | TETETETETETEQ | 22 |
| 23. | LAAAAAAAEK | 14 |

| | | |
|---|---|---:|
| 24. | LLAAAAAAAEK | 15 |
| 25. | LLLAAAAAAAEK | 17 |
| 26. | LLLLAAAAAAAEK | 17 |
| 27. | ANIZ | 26 |
| 28. | UANIZ | 14 |
| 29. | SUANIZ | 15 |
| 30. | USUANIZ | 16 |
| 31. | SUSUANIZ | 18 |
| 32. | USUSUANIZ | 18 |
| 33. | SUSUSUANIZ | 19 |
| 34. | USUSUSUANIZ | 20 |
| 35. | SUSUSUSUANIZ | 42 |
| 36. | *SUSUSUSUANIZ | 21 |
| 37. | OOOOOOO, OTETETETETEQ, OLLLLAAAAAAAEK | 100 |
| 38. | BD, DO | 8 |
| 39. | CC, CO, CO | 14 |
| 40. | CCM, MO | 13 |
| 41. | PP, PO | 10 |
| 42. | PPD | 8 |
| 43. | RROOOOOOORRORR, BR, PR, DR, O*SUSUSUSUANIZ | 153 |
| 44. | BBDJCCMMPPDXGGG, BR, JOTETETETETEQ, MOLLLLAAAAAAAEK, XO*SUSUSUSUANIZ, GR, GR | 1,990 |
| | Total | 5,876 |

One tile, a blank (indicated by an asterisk), was left in the rack at the end of the game.

Can you improve on this score? Finding the highest score for a complete game, as opposed to a single move, is *not* an easy problem to solve.

| | | | | | | | | | | | | | | |
|---|---|---|---|---|---|---|---|---|---|---|---|---|---|---|
| B | R | | 2L | | | 3W | | | | 2L | | | I | F |
| B | R | | | | 3L | | | | 3L | | | | I | F |
| D | O | 2W | | | 2L | | 2L | | | | | I | E | V |
| J | O | T | E | T | E | T | E | T | E | T | E | T | E | Q |
| C | O | | | 2W | | | | | 2W | | | I | E | H |
| C | O | | | | 3L | | | | 3L | | | N | E | H |
| M | O | 2L | | | 2L | | 2L | | | | | N | E | V |
| M | O | L | L | L | L | A | A | A | A | A | A | A | E | K |
| P | O | 2L | | | 2L | | 2L | | | | | N | E | W |
| P | R | | | 3L | | | | 3L | | | | N | I | W |
| D | R | | 2W | | | | | 2W | | | | A | I | Y |
| X | O | + | S | U | S | U | S | U | S | U | A | N | I | Z |
| G | R | 2W | | | 2L | | 2L | | | | | N | I | Y |
| G | R | | | 3L | | | | 3L | | | | | I | D |
| G | | 2L | | | | 3W | | | | 2L | | | | D |

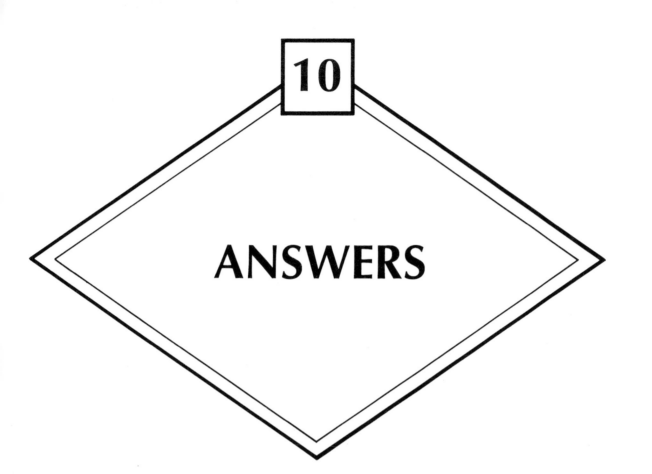

10

ANSWERS

# SOLUTIONS TO SCRABBLE PUZZLES

1. Play ROUNDEL and STAGE for 88 points.
2. Using the L of JOLLY, play PETROLIC for 70 points.
3. Using the S of RETURNS, play GLASSINE, DA and ES for 79 points.
4. Using the Z of CHEZ, and using the blank as a Q, play QUATORZE for 203 points.
5. Using the blank as an S, play FAITHWORTHINESS and CALLS for an incredible 773 points! The blank must be the first of the two Ss in FAITHWORTHINESS.
6. Play BOXFULS, XEROTIC and SHALLOWS for 180 points.
7. Play MYTHS and TOE for 54 points.
8. Play EVZONE and OAT for 47 points.
9. Using the blanks as an S and an I, play STEARIN, RET and TARE for 71 points.
10. Using the blank as an R, play QINTARS and TEEN for 104 points.
11. Using the blank as an E, play SISSIES and QUACKS for 134 points.
12. Using the blank as an S, play PHLOXES, EXPORT, ME and IS for 154 points.
13. Play VODKA and VILL for 57 points.
14. Play JIHAD and DRUM for 43 points.
15. Play AUREI, DOR and HE for 19 points.
16. Using the O of EBON, play BODYWORK for 108 points. Note that the O of EBON must be the first O of BODYWORK to score 108 points.
17. Play ADIEU or OIDIA, and DATE, for 17 points.
18. Either: play ERGATES and EON for 73 points, with either E of ERGATES corresponding to the E of EON; or: play RESTAGE and EON for 73 points, with the second E of RESTAGE and the E of EON corresponding.
19. Play ERYNGO and SPAY for 55 points.
20. Using the A of ENTAIL, play WAVEBAND for 118 points.
21. Either: play CHARK and MANIAC for 68 points; or: play KETCH and BARK for 68 points.
22. Play CRUSADO, WENDS and LIDO for 76 points.
23. Using the X of EXHAUSTS, play RONDEAUX for 86 points.
24. Play SCHLEPP, STARRING, HEARTH, ELECTOR and PREGNANT for 135 points.
25. Using the blank as a Z, play ZYMURGY, MAY, MARCH, TEAR and TOY for 99 points.

# SOLUTIONS TO PUZZLES WITH A THEME

1. Using the second A of ARGALI, play CAPYBARA for 96 points.
2. Using the N of SERIN, and using the blank as an F, play FLAMINGO for 72 points.
3. Using the first E of GREEN, play BEIGE for 16 points.
4. Using the E of DHOLE, and using the blanks as an L and a K, play ELKHOUND for 59 points.
5. Using the first S of SCHEMERS, and using the blank as an S or a T, play EXEGESES or EXEGETES for 96 points.
6. Using the R of SANDER, and using the blank as an H, play THRASHER for 149 points.
7. Using the blanks as a C and an S, play CASSINO and SNAP for 70 points.
8. Using the blanks as a T and a Y, play TIMOTHY and JOEY for 96 points.
9. Play ZOOS and THRONGS for 34 points.
10. Using the first O of POTATO, play COLZA for 44 points.

# SOLUTIONS TO 100 ANAGRAMS

| | | | |
|---|---|---|---|
| 1. AERATES | 21. ANOESIS | 41. NEONATE | 61. TESTIER |
| 2. RALLINE | 22. ROSELLA | 42. AREOLAR | 62. LINNETS |
| 3. ATELIER | 23. ASSURES | 43. ARREARS | 63. TOLLERS |
| 4. LAITIES | 24. TAUNTER | 44. EASIEST | 64. SNORTER |
| 5. SIERRAN | 25. SIRLOIN | 45. ALUNITE | 65. ANATASE |
| 6. ETESIAN | 26. SERIATE | 46. SITUATE | 66. AREOLAE |
| 7. AIRIEST | 27. NAILERS | 47. ULULATE | 67. AUREOLA |
| 8. ORLEANS | 28. LITERAL | 48. TENANTS | 68. LARIATS |
| 9. NEUTRAL | 29. TALLIES | 49. LEISURE | 69. LEARNER |
| 10. ELUANTS | 30. INERTIA | 50. TENUOUS | 70. NANNIES |
| 11. ROASTER | 31. ISATINE | 51. ROSEATE | 71. LLANERO |
| 12. RESENTS | 32. OTARIES | 52. AERIALS | 72. ROULEAU |
| 13. SNIRTLE | 33. RANSELS | 53. TERTIAL | 73. ENTITLE |
| 14. LENTORS | 34. SEALANT | 54. ISOLATE | 74. AUTUERS |
| 15. UNRESTS | 35. OESTRAL | 55. ENTRAIN | 75. NEUTRON |
| 16. TALARIA | 36. EERIEST | 56. ATONIES | 76. AUSTERE |
| 17. NEATEST | 37. TENSILE | 57. ARSENAL | 77. REALISE |
| 18. NARRATE | 38. STOITER | 58. LANTERN | 78. URALITE |
| 19. AREOLES | 39. ENROOTS | 59. STANNEL | 79. ERASION |
| 20. ELATION | 40. AUREATE | 60. SALUTER | 80. OTARINE |

| | | | |
|---|---|---|---|
| 81. ATRESIA | 86. RELENTS | 91. ARIETTA | 96. TALLENT |
| 82. LANNERS | 87. LINTIES | 92. ERASURE | 97. TONNEAU |
| 83. TRENTAL | 88. TOLTERS | 93. ALIENEE | 98. TRANTER |
| 84. ETALONS | 89. RUNLETS | 94. LIAISES | 99. LANOLIN |
| 85. TANNERS | 90. ALIASES | 95. ENATION | 100. NOURSLE |

# SOLUTIONS TO ANOTHER 100 ANAGRAMS

| | | | |
|---|---|---|---|
| 1. REDDENS | 26. SILAGED | 51. IDEATES | 76. LINEAGE |
| 2. GUINEAS | 27. DANDERS | 52. ORIGANE | 77. DEASOIL |
| 3. DARTLES | 28. AGEINGS | 53. LEGLANS | 78. LAGGENS |
| 4. NAIADES | 29. ENDORSE | 54. STANDER | 79. AGAINST |
| 5. RANTING | 30. STRIDES | 55. SIRGANG | 80. GENTILE |
| 6. AGNISED | 31. GREISEN | 56. DINNERS | 81. TELLING |
| 7. TARRING | 32. TRUEING | 57. GENITOR | 82. IGNITES |
| 8. INSURED | 33. ANGLERS | 58. AGISTED | 83. RATTING |
| 9. TANGLES | 34. DANDIES | 59. GLASSEN | 84. GEARING |
| 10. RESIDUA | 35. LARGEST | 60. GENDERS | 85. ANISEED |
| 11. DAUTIES | 36. ORATING | 61. LENTIGO | 86. RENDERS |
| 12. SINGLES | 37. RATLING | 62. DOGTROT | 87. TINDERS |
| 13. AGNISES | 38. SNARING | 63. LUNGIES | 88. STIRRED |
| 14. AGONIST | 39. ELUTING | 64. INSIDER | 89. GUNITES |
| 15. DENTILS | 40. TONNAGE | 65. GODSONS | 90. DEGRADE |
| 16. ARDUOUS | 41. ILLEGAL | 66. NUDISTS | 91. DOTINGS |
| 17. SLEDGES | 42. DEGAUSS | 67. GEORDIE | 92. ANGULAR |
| 18. GOATEES | 43. OUTDATE | 68. DRAGGED | 93. GONDOLA |
| 19. GLOATED | 44. DILATED | 69. TREATED | 94. DOGGONE |
| 20. AUDITED | 45. OUTDOOR | 70. ALLEGRO | 95. DULLING |
| 21. RETUNDS | 46. ORDINAL | 71. DOSAGES | 96. DISGUST |
| 22. DEADENS | 47. DELETED | 72. STALAGS | 97. NODULES |
| 23. DOULEIA | 48. DOGGING | 73. GADDING | 98. GRASSES |
| 24. EULOGIA | 49. GESTATE | 74. ALLEGED | 99. DILUTED |
| 25. AUDIENT | 50. AUDITOR | 75. RIDINGS | 100. ADENOID |

# SOLUTIONS TO A FURTHER 100 ANAGRAMS

| | | | |
|---|---|---|---|
| 1. MISDATE | 5. SOAPING | 9. WESTERN | 13. MELTING |
| 2. MARGINS | 6. ATEBRIN | 10. HERDENS | 14. STERNUM |
| 3. SHADIER | 7. DECERNS | 11. BENDERS | 15. BAILERS |
| 4. RAVINES | 8. BINGLES | 12. SWEATER | 16. RAPINES |

| | | | |
|---|---|---|---|
| 17. VENTILS | 38. SYRINGE | 59. HEALING | 80. CEASING |
| 18. SASHING | 39. RESPITE | 60. BELTING | 81. LEAVING |
| 19. HERBIST | 40. FASTING | 61. ORGANIC | 82. DISABLE |
| 20. BESTING | 41. TEMSING | 62. SELFING | 83. VENDERS |
| 21. REBITES | 42. BRANTLE | 63. REPEATS | 84. MENDERS |
| 22. CENTRAL | 43. PETROLS | 64. WEARING | 85. MEALING |
| 23. DACITES | 44. REAPING | 65. COASTER | 86. FELTING |
| 24. PLANERS | 45. TRIABLE | 66. BASHING | 87. SABRING |
| 25. INVADES | 46. WAILERS | 67. REVISAL | 88. FALTERS |
| 26. PLAITER | 47. PINDERS | 68. WASTREL | 89. GIANTRY |
| 27. BASTING | 48. PAUSING | 69. STAVING | 90. VESTING |
| 28. FAIREST | 49. CRINGES | 70. WANTERS | 91. POSTERN |
| 29. BRACING | 50. REALITY | 71. SORBENT | 92. LEVANTS |
| 30. CARLINE | 51. BANGLES | 72. SPANGLE | 93. DIALYSE |
| 31. MINGLES | 52. DANCERS | 73. GERMINS | 94. SPENDER |
| 32. PANDERS | 53. MILTERS | 74. VENTRAL | 95. HEARING |
| 33. FENDERS | 54. WANGLES | 75. FEARING | 96. ANGUISH |
| 34. PASTING | 55. PASSING | 76. SPADING | 97. BARITES |
| 35. BANTERS | 56. RAVELIN | 77. FLANGES | 98. DEVISAL |
| 36. PARLIES | 57. STAYING | 78. HALIDES | 99. HIRSUTE |
| 37. SALFERN | 58. ENCRUST | 79. BEARING | 100. PELTING |

# SOLUTIONS TO YET ANOTHER 100 ANAGRAMS

| | | | |
|---|---|---|---|
| 1. JAILERS | 21. AZOTISE | 41. JOINTED | 61. SERKALI |
| 2. KANDIES | 22. ZOOLITE | 42. KNARRED | 62. KNITTED |
| 3. LAZIEST | 23. QUARTER | 43. EXARATE | 63. ADJOINT |
| 4. DARKENS | 24. ADJOURN | 44. EXUDATE | 64. ZONATED |
| 5. KERNITE | 25. EXEDRAE | 45. QUININE | 65. QUARTOS |
| 6. JINGLET | 26. ZELANTS | 46. QUIETUS | 66. AXILLAE |
| 7. KURSAAL | 27. QUARREL | 47. ZEALANT | 67. QUASSIA |
| 8. KINGLES | 28. STONKER | 48. ZOISITE | 68. ZOONITE |
| 9. JINGLER | 29. ZINGELS | 49. QUITTOR | 69. QUILTER |
| 10. STOKING | 30. ZANIEST | 50. EXIGENT | 70. EXORDIA |
| 11. REDSKIN | 31. TAXINGS | 51. JADEITE | 71. ZONULET |
| 12. JANTIES | 32. RANKLES | 52. KARTING | 72. AZURITE |
| 13. SINKAGE | 33. JOLTERS | 53. RANZELS | 73. JOTTING |
| 14. JANGLER | 34. ZANDERS | 54. KIDDIES | 74. KGOTLAS |
| 15. KINESIS | 35. JINGLES | 55. KINGLET | 75. EXTENSE |
| 16. AXINITE | 36. KALENDS | 56. KNOTTER | 76. QUADRAT |
| 17. KETONES | 37. EXTERNS | 57. SKAILED | 77. SEXTUOR |
| 18. QUINTAL | 38. DZERENS | 58. SNAKIER | 78. SKIRTED |
| 19. EXALTED | 39. QUARTAN | 59. QUANNET | 79. INTAKES |
| 20. JARRING | 40. JITTERS | 60. LANKIER | 80. KERATIN |

| 81. JANGLES | 86. KESTREL | 91. JANITOR | 96. XEROSIS |
| 82. JESSANT | 87. KEITLOA | 92. KENOSIS | 97. JAUNTIE |
| 83. JESTING | 88. ZEOLITE | 93. ZORILLE | 98. QUIETEN |
| 84. LANKEST | 89. JUTTING | 94. XERASIA | 99. JUGULAR |
| 85. JOINDER | 90. KEELSON | 95. QUARTET | 100. EXTERNE |

# SOLUTIONS TO THE LAST 100 ANAGRAMS

| 1. KINGDOM | 26. QUICKEN | 51. LOZENGE | 76. ROYALTY |
| 2. MYSTIFY | 27. FIBBING | 52. OFFHAND | 77. GIMMICK |
| 3. NAPHTHA | 28. PROVERB | 53. KILLJOY | 78. IDYLLIC |
| 4. ORGANZA | 29. EMBLAZE | 54. QUANTUM | 79. LITHIUM |
| 5. ZESTFUL | 30. FUCHSIA | 55. INQUIRY | 80. OVERTAX |
| 6. KIBBUTZ | 31. MIDWIFE | 56. CHUTNEY | 81. PHALANX |
| 7. GYMNAST | 32. ALCOHOL | 57. ISTHMUS | 82. YELLOWY |
| 8. GHERKIN | 33. MASTIFF | 58. OCTAGON | 83. KEYHOLE |
| 9. PLYWOOD | 34. LENGTHY | 59. ZINCIFY | 84. EQUINOX |
| 10. RHUBARB | 35. FOXHOLE | 60. ROCKERY | 85. HYGIENE |
| 11. ZOOLOGY | 36. GRAPHIC | 61. MUGWUMP | 86. LIQUEFY |
| 12. BOXWOOD | 37. PYRAMID | 62. INFANCY | 87. NOVELTY |
| 13. FIXEDLY | 38. ECOLOGY | 63. ABYSMAL | 88. HEXAGON |
| 14. YOUNGLY | 39. SCRAWNY | 64. VOMITED | 89. BRONZED |
| 15. UNCOUTH | 40. QUIESCE | 65. SAFFRON | 90. YASHMAK |
| 16. JACKDAW | 41. THRIFTY | 66. HOBNAIL | 91. BASHFUL |
| 17. DONKEYS | 42. TRAPEZE | 67. ANTHRAX | 92. NAKEDLY |
| 18. VACANCY | 43. DWARFED | 68. TYPHOID | 93. WOMANLY |
| 19. UPGRADE | 44. JONQUIL | 69. WHITISH | 94. JAYWALK |
| 20. COXCOMB | 45. DYNASTY | 70. RAWHIDE | 95. QUIBBLE |
| 21. JUSTIFY | 46. VARIETY | 71. SYMPTOM | 96. BOROUGH |
| 22. UNSWEPT | 47. CZARDOM | 72. TYRANNY | 97. AWKWARD |
| 23. SHADOWY | 48. ZANYISM | 73. EXACTLY | 98. UNGODLY |
| 24. YAWNING | 49. CRAZILY | 74. WARPATH | 99. NETWORK |
| 25. VOLCANO | 50. HIGHWAY | 75. WAXWORK | 100. DOGFISH |

# SOLUTION TO EIGHT EIGHTS

The total score is 865 points, made up of:

| SAMIZDAT | 140 points | BEPUFFED | 88 points |
| DYSLEXIC | 124 points | CHOLIAMB | 77 points |
| RHAPSODY | 92 points | LAWGIVER | 70 points |
| JARARAKA | 104 points | VERQUIRE | 140 points |

## SOLUTIONS TO IMPROPER NAMES

| | | | |
|---|---|---|---|
| 1. AUGUST | 14. GLORIA | 27. LUCIFER | 40. SURREY |
| 2. BERLIN | 15. GUERNSEY | 28. LULU | 41. TEXAS |
| 3. BOSTON | 16. HARROW | 29. MAC | 42. TRIPOLI |
| 4. CHILE | 17. HENRY | 30. MARTINI | 43. ULSTER |
| 5. CHINA | 18. HOLLAND | 31. MOROCCO | 44. VESTA |
| 6. DUTCH | 19. ILIAD | 32. NELSON | 45. VESUVIAN |
| 7. EASTER | 20. JAPAN | 33. NEWTON | 46. WALES |
| 8. ETNA | 21. JERSEY | 34. PACIFIC | 47. WELSH |
| 9. EURO | 22. KELVIN | 35. ROENTGEN | 48. XENIA |
| 10. FARADAY | 23. KENT | 36. ROMAN | 49. YANK |
| 11. FULHAM | 24. LIMA | 37. SCOTCH | 50. YONKERS |
| 12. GENEVA | 25. LIMBO | 38. SCOTIA | |
| 13. GERMAN | 26. LIMERICK | 39. SIAMESE | |

# SOLUTIONS TO A PUZZLING POT POURRI

**1.**

AGINST combines with 21 different letters. Examples of possible words are:

| | | | | | |
|---|---|---|---|---|---|
| A | AGAINST | H | HASTING | R | STARING |
| B | BASTING | K | SKATING | T | STATING |
| C | CASTING | L | LASTING | U | SAUTING |
| D | DATINGS | M | MASTING | V | STAVING |
| E | TEASING | N | STANING | W | WASTING |
| F | FASTING | O | AGONIST | X | TAXINGS |
| G | STAGING | P | PASTING | Y | STAYING |

**2.**

GJU is a kind of violin from the Shetland Islands.

**3.**

HOLIDAY and HYALOID.

**4.**

A total of 325 points is possible. The following moves are made:

| | | |
|---|---|---|
| 1. | FA | 10 |
| 2. | HA, HE | 18 |
| 3. | HAD | 9 |
| 4. | HADJ | 17 |
| 5. | HADJI | 18 |
| 6. | ME | 10 |
| 7. | BLOCKING | 118 |
| 8. | BLOCKINGS | 18 |
| 9. | HET | 6 |
| 10. | CUR | 5 |
| 11. | CURVY | 13 |
| 12. | PYX | 45 |
| 13. | FAW, MEW | 17 |
| 14. | ZO | 31 |
| | minus unused letters | −10 |
| | **Total** | **325** |

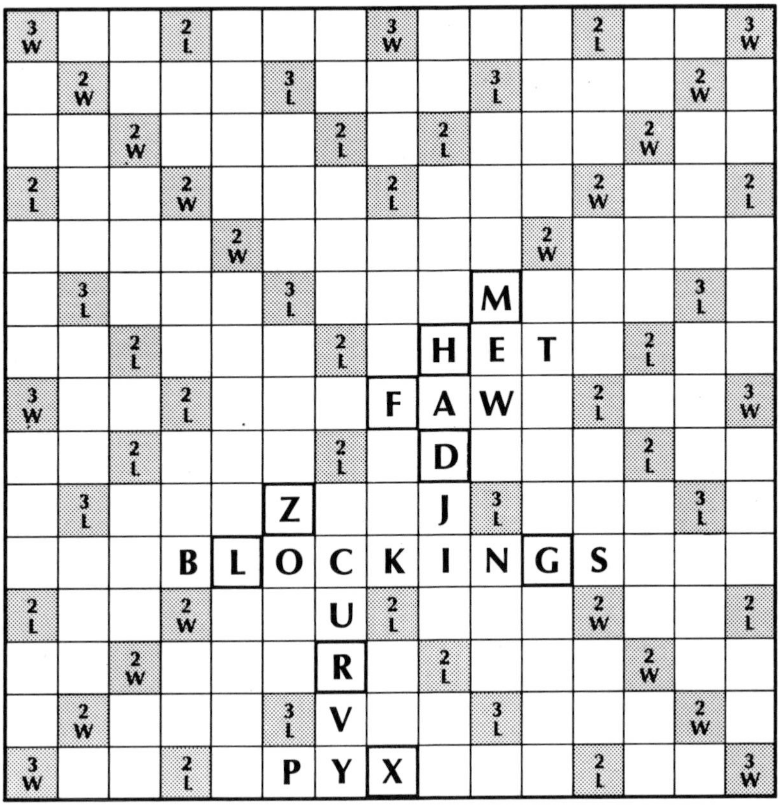
M
H E T
F A W
D
Z J
B L O C K I N G S
U
R
V
P Y X

**5.**
The word ILL can have 18 different letters added in front of it: B, C, D, F, G, H, J, K, L, M, N, P, R, S, T, V, W and Y.

**6.**
DOUBTER, OBTRUDE, OUTBRED and REDOUBT.

**7.**
SISTRUM and TRISMUS.

**8.**
The largest rectangle is one measuring 10 squares by 3 squares, a total of 30 squares. The three horizontal words involved are CORDIALISE, ORIENTATES and LEANNESSES; the ten vertical words are COL, ORE, RIA, DEN, INN, ATE, LAS, ITS, SEE and ESS.

```
C O R D I A L I S E
O R I E N T A T E S
L E A N N E S S E S
```

**9.**

EGIJLN combines with six different letters.

| | | | | | | |
|---|---|---|---|---|---|---|
| D | JINGLED | L | JELLING | S | JINGLES |
| E | JEELING | R | JINGLER | T | JINGLET |

**10.**

DOULEIA, MOINEAU and SEQUOIA.

**11.**

DIALOGUE, DOULEIAS, EDACIOUS, EQUATION, EUPHORIA, MOINEAUS, ODALIQUE and SEQUOIAS.

**12.**

In the game shown here, 1,334 points have been scored. The words played are as follows:

| | | |
|---|---|---|
| 1. | STRANDS (A = blank) | 68 |
| 2. | ARBLAST, ST | 66 |
| 3. | YARDWAND | 230 |
| 4. | ALB | 10 |
| 5. | AN | 2 |
| 6. | VAN | 6 |
| 7. | VANG | 16 |
| 8. | ATTRACTS | 72 |
| 9. | FLAPJACK | 356 |
| 10. | AM | 10 |
| 11. | LA | 2 |
| 12. | LAX | 10 |
| 13. | FLAX | 28 |
| 14. | GRANNAMS (both As = blanks) | 65 |
| 15. | VAN | 10 |
| 16. | VANG | 7 |
| 17. | TWA, ST | 8 |
| 18. | HA | 5 |
| 19. | HAPHAZARD | 383 |
| | Total | 1,334 |

| | | | | | | | | | | | | | | |
|---|---|---|---|---|---|---|---|---|---|---|---|---|---|---|
| 3W | | | 2L | | | F | L | A | P | J | A | C | K | |
| | 2W | | | 3L | | | | M | | | T | 2W | | |
| | | 2W | | | 2L | | 2L | | | | T | | | |
| 2L | | | 2W | | | 2L | | | 2W | | R | | 2L | |
| | | | | 2W | | | | | F | L | A | X | | |
| | 3L | | | 3L | | | G | | | | C | 3L | | |
| | | 2L | | | 2L | | 2L | R | | | T | | | |
| Y | | 2L | V | | S | T | R | + | N | D | S | | | 3W |
| A | R | B | L | A | S | T | | 2L | N | | | 2L | | |
| A | R | 3L | | N | 3L | | | N | | | | 3L | | |
| D | | | G | | | V | + | N | G | | | | | |
| W | | | 2W | | | 2L | | M | | 2W | | | 2L | |
| A | L | B | | | 2L | | 2L | S | T | | 2W | | | |
| N | 2W | | | 3L | | | 3L | W | | | 2W | | | |
| D | | | 2L | | H | A | P | H | A | Z | A | R | D | |

**13.**

ATINGLE, ELATING, GELATIN and GENITAL.

**14.**

CABBAGE is just one of many possibilities.

**15.**

A score of 2,639 is possible. Play the words as follows:

| | | |
|---|---|---|
| 1. | HAGGLER | 76 |
| 2. | ANNATTO, HO | 65 |
| 3. | NATRIUM, MHO (U = blank) | 73 |
| 4. | VOWELIZE | 142 |
| 5. | OBLIVION (L = blank) | 80 |
| 6. | EXPIRED, DO | 93 |
| 7. | ROULEAU, OX, UP, LI, ER, AE, UDO | 104 |

| F | R | E | Q | U | E | N | T | A | T | I | V | E | L | Y |
|---|---|---|---|---|---|---|---|---|---|---|---|---|---|---|
|  | O | X |  | M | ³ᴸ | A |  | N | ³ᴸ | C |  | N | O |  |
|  | U | P |  | B |  | T |  | N |  | T |  | G | O |  |
| ²ᴸ | L | I | ²ᵂ | R |  | R | ²ᴸ | A |  | E | ²ᵂ | I | F | ²ᴸ |
|  | E | R |  | O |  | I |  | T |  | R |  | N | A |  |
|  | A | E |  | U | ³ᴸ | + |  | T | ³ᴸ | I |  | E | H |  |
| J | U | D | O | S |  | M | H | O |  | C | A | D | S |  |
| A |  |  | B |  |  |  | A |  |  |  | P |  |  | ³ᵂ |
| Y |  | ²ᴸ | + |  | ²ᴸ | G | ²ᴸ |  |  | S | ²ᴸ |  |  |  |
| W | ³ᴸ |  | I | ³ᴸ |  | G |  | ³ᴸ |  | I |  | ³ᴸ |  |  |
| A |  |  | V | O | W | E | L | I | Z | E | D |  |  |  |
| L |  |  | I |  |  | E |  |  |  | E |  |  |  | ²ᴸ |
| K |  | ²ᵂ | O |  | ²ᴸ | R | ²ᴸ |  |  | S | ²ᵂ |  |  |  |
| E | ²ᵂ |  | N | ³ᴸ |  |  | ³ᴸ |  |  |  | ²ᵂ |  |  |  |
| D |  |  | ²ᴸ |  | ³ᵂ |  |  |  | ²ᴸ |  |  | ³ᵂ |  |  |

**16.**

The very first alphabetically reduced form is AAAALTY, from the word ATALAYA. The last alphabetically reduced form is ORSTTUU, from the word SURTOUT.

**17.**
BALMIER, MIRABLE and REMBLAI.

**18.**
SPONSOR is one of a few examples.

**19.**
Using the two blanks as a D and an N, arrange the tiles in the symmetrical pattern shown here.

```
S Q U A N + E R I + G
  P   G I E   W U D   E
  O W   L A V E D   E R
  R I B   T A S   F O R
  O G L E   N   V I N Y
  C   O A F ☆ P I X   M
  Y A K S   T   Z E T A
  S H E   J U T   D U N
  T A   L I B E L   I D
  I   O O N   A I A   E
  C H R O N O M E T E R
```

**20.**

| | | | |
|---|---|---|---|
| JAMBEUX | ASPHYXY | POSTFIX | UPWHIRL |
| BAWDKIN | DVORNIK | KRYPSIS | LYOPHIL |
| FINNSKO | ISCHIUM | GYTRASH | QUONDAM |
| RHYTINA | MYALGIC | ECTHYMA | XIPHOID |
| WHITLOW | SCRANCH | CROPFUL | THATCHT |
| ZARNICH | VITRAUX | ONYMOUS | HEXAPOD |
| NYMPHIC | YAKHDAN | | |

**21.**

The key word in devising the high-scoring solution here is UEY, an Australian colloquialism for a U-turn. That word appears in the 1983 edition of *Chambers Twentieth Century Dictionary*. A score of 117 points is possible from the board set-up shown here. Playing the Q to the left of UEYS creates the vertical word LACQUEYS and the horizontal word QUEYS.

| | | | | | | | | | | | | | | |
|---|---|---|---|---|---|---|---|---|---|---|---|---|---|---|
| 3W | | | 2L | | | | 3W | | | | 2L | | | 3W |
| | 2W | | | | 3L | | | 3L | | | | 2W | | |
| | | 2W | | | | 2L | | 2L | | | | 2W | | |
| 2L | | | 2W | | | | 2L | | | | 2W | | | 2L |
| L | | | | 2W | | | | | 2W | | | | | |
| A | 3L | | | | 3L | | | 3L | | | | 3L | | |
| C | O | R | E | | | 2L | | 2L | | | | 2L | | |
| U (3W) | E | Y | S | | | | T | | | | 2L | | | 3W |
| U | T | 2L | E | | | 2L | I | 2L | | | | 2L | | |
| E | 3L | | D | R | A | I | N | | 3L | | | | 3L | |
| Y | | | | 2W | | | | | 2W | | | | | |
| S | | 2W | | | | 2L | | | | 2W | | | | 2L |
| | 2W | | | | 2L | | 2L | | | | 2W | | | |
| | 2W | | | 3L | | | | 3L | | | | 2W | | |
| 3W | | | 2L | | | | 3W | | | | 2L | | | 3W |

**22.**

CHEMICAL is a common word in this category.

**23.**

CERAMET, CREMATE and MEERCAT.

**24.**

Assume player one picks up ZQJXHVY, and player two picks up FFHKVWW. Neither player can go, so the game is finished before it really starts! Each player's score is reduced from zero by the value of the letters on that player's rack. Thus, a final score of *minus* 48 to *minus* 29 is achieved. Even in a game where the number of times a player can change his letters is limited, the same situation can arise.

**25.**

| | | | | | | | |
|---|---|---|---|---|---|---|---|
| D | CRASHED | K | HACKERS | O | ROACHES | T | RATCHES |
| E | REACHES | L | LARCHES | P | PARCHES | U | ARCHEUS |
| F | CHAFERS | M | MARCHES | R | ARCHERS | V | VARECHS |
| G | CHARGES | N | RANCHES | S | CRASHES | X | EXARCHS |
| I | CASHIER | | | | | | |

**26.**

In the game shown here, 1,664 points have been scored. The words played are as follows:

| | |
|---|---:|
| 1. STRETCH | 80 |
| 2. ER | 2 |
| 3. FRECKLE, ERR (first E = blank) | 74 |
| 4. WHEEZLED | 356 |
| 5. STRENGTH | 76 |
| 6. ESS | 4 |
| 7. NESS | 4 |
| 8. EN | 2 |
| 9. BENJ | 42 |
| 10. ENDS (E = blank) | 6 |
| 11. FETTLER, RENDS | 83 |
| 12. ME | 4 |
| 13. MEW, WE | 12 |
| 14. EMMEW | 18 |
| 15. EX | 9 |
| 16. WEB | 7 |
| 17. GED | 5 |
| 18. EGGED | 16 |
| 19. ER | 2 |
| 20. PERPLEXEDNESSES | 860 |
| 21. EN | 2 |
| | |
| Total | 1,664 |

Grid (Scrabble-style):

Row 1: P E R P L E X E D N E S S E S
Row 2: G M N 3L T 2W
Row 3: G 2W M 2L 2L R
Row 4: F E T T L E R 2L B E N J
Row 5: D 2W W + B 2W N
Row 6: 3L 3L N 3L G 3L
Row 7: 2L D 2L T
Row 8: 3W 2L S T R E T C H W
Row 9: 2L 2L 2L R 2L H
Row 10: 3L 3L F R + C K L E
Row 11: 2W 2W E
Row 12: 2L 2W 2L 2W Z
Row 13: 2W 2L 2L 2W L
Row 14: 2W 3L 3L 2W E
Row 15: 3W 2L 3W 2L D

**27.**

| | | | |
|---|---|---|---|
| LAUNDER | ARCADING | RETCHES | ANCESTRAL |
| ETHANOL | CAUTIONERS | SORTED | DOMINATES |
| ASTHENICS | LEACHES | STASHING | THROWING |

**28.**

MEDICABLE is one such word.

**29.**

| | | | |
|---|---|---|---|
| BBBELRU | (BLUBBER) | IIIKMNN | (MINIKIN) |
| CCCNOOT | (CONCOCT) | JNOORSU | (SOJOURN) |
| DDDESTU | (STUDDED) | KLLMOSU | (MOLLUSK) |
| EEEEFRR | (REFEREE) | LLMPPUY | (PLUMPLY) |
| FFGIINR | (GRIFFIN) | MMNOSSU | (SUMMONS) |
| GGGIINR | (RIGGING) | NNOOOPT | (PONTOON) |
| HHIIPPS | (HIPPISH) | | |

## 30.

AEINST is a fertile set of six letters.

| | | | | | |
|---|---|---|---|---|---|
| B | BESTAIN | J | JANTIES | S | ENTASIS |
| C | CINEAST | K | INTAKES | T | INSTATE |
| D | INSTEAD | L | SALIENT | U | AUNTIES |
| E | ETESIAN | M | INMATES | V | NATIVES |
| F | FAINEST | O | ATONIES | W | TAWNIES |
| G | SEATING | P | PANTIES | Z | ZANIEST |
| I | ISATINE | R | NASTIER | | |

## 31.

It is possible to play ZO for 158 points, making the words BAMBOOZLED and PSYCHOPHYSICS at the same time. In the diagram here, play ZO horizontally in the two right hand columns. The individual word scores are: ZO – 33, BAMBOOZLED – 26, and PSYCHOPHYSICS – 99.

| | | | | | | | | | | | | | | |
|---|---|---|---|---|---|---|---|---|---|---|---|---|---|---|
| 3W | | | 2L | | | | 3W | | | | 2L | | | 3W |
| | 2W | | | | 3L | | | | 3L | | | | B | |
| | | 2W | | | | 2L | | 2L | | | | T | A | P |
| 2L | | | 2W | | | | 2L | | | | R | A | M | S |
| | | | | 2W | | | | | | 2W | U | | B | Y |
| | 3L | | | | 3L | | | | M | A | N | I | O | C |
| | | 2L | | | | 2L | | 2L | I | | | 2L | O | H |
| 3W | | | 2L | | | D | A | R | N | | 2L | | | 3W |
| | | 2L | | | | 2L | | 2L | E | | H | E | L | P |
| | 3L | | | | 3L | | | | D | U | O | | E | H |
| 2L | | | | 2W | | | 2L | | | M | O | O | D | Y |
| | | | 2W | | 2L | | | | 2L | | K | | | S |
| | | 2W | | | | 2L | | 2L | | | | 2W | | I |
| | 2W | | | | 3L | | | | 3L | | | | 2W | C |
| 3W | | | 2L | | | | 3W | | | | 2L | | | S |

**32.**
AEQRSU combines with eight different letters.

| | | | |
|---|---|---|---|
| B | BARQUES | R | SQUARER |
| D | SQUARED | S | SQUARES |
| E | QUAERES | T | QUARTES |
| M | MARQUES | V | QUAVERS |

**33.**
TORTUOUS is a common example.

**34.**
BILLOWY is in most dictionaries.

**35.**
IMPANEL and MANIPLE.

**36.**

| | | | |
|---|---|---|---|
| AQRTUYZ | (QUARTZY) | HRSSTUY | (THYRSUS) |
| BOOPSTY | (POSTBOY) | IPRSTUU | (PURSUIT) |
| CORRSUY | (CURSORY) | JNOORSU | (SOJOURN) |
| DOOPRSY | (PROSODY) | KOORTUW | (OUTWORK) |
| ERSTTTU | (STUTTER) | LPRSSUU | (SURPLUS) |
| FORRUWY | (FURROWY) | MORRSTU | (ROSTRUM) |
| GOORTUW | (OUTGROW) | NOPSSTU | (SUNSPOT) |

**37.**
TEWHITS, WETTISH and WHITEST.

**38.**
The longest common word with its letters in typewriter order is WETTISH. This word is also one of the solutions to question 37.

**39.**
DAMAGEABLE is one such word.

**40.**
In the game shown here, 1,256 points have been scored. The words played are as follows:

| # | Word | Score |
|---|------|-------|
| 1. | STRINGS (I = blank) | 66 |
| 2. | IMPRINTS | 76 |
| 3. | HI | 5 |
| 4. | WHIFFLING | 284 |
| 5. | MI | 4 |
| 6. | MIX | 12 |
| 7. | MIXT | 26 |
| 8. | TWIBILL, ST (second I = blank) | 65 |
| 9. | BLITZING | 320 |
| 10. | IT | 2 |
| 11. | RIT | 3 |
| 12. | DIRNDLS, RITS | 94 |
| 13. | IN | 2 |
| 14. | INDRI | 8 |
| 15. | HI | 5 |
| 16. | DIPCHICKS | 284 |
| | **Total** | **1,256** |

| | | | | | | | | | | | | | | |
|---|---|---|---|---|---|---|---|---|---|---|---|---|---|---|
| W |   |   | 2L |   |   |   | 3W |   |   |   | 2L |   |   | D |
| H | 2W |   |   | M | 3L |   |   | 3L |   |   |   | 2W |   | I |
| I | M | P | R | I | N | T | S | 2L |   |   |   | 2W |   | P |
| F |   | 2W |   | X |   |   | T |   |   |   | 2W |   |   | C |
| F |   |   |   | T |   |   | R |   | D |   |   |   |   | H |
| L | 3L |   |   |   | 3L |   | + | 3L | I | N | D | R | I | I |
| I |   | 2L |   |   | 2L |   | N | 2L | R |   | 2L |   |   | C |
| N |   |   | 2L |   |   |   | G |   | N | 2L |   |   |   | K |
| G | 2L |   |   |   | 2L |   | S | T | D |   | 2L |   |   | S |
|   | 3L |   |   | 3L |   |   |   | W | L |   |   |   | 3L |   |
|   |   |   | 2W |   |   |   | R | I | T | S |   |   |   |   |
| 2L |   |   | 2W |   |   | 2L |   | B |   |   | 2W |   |   | 2L |
|   |   | 2W |   |   | 2L |   |   | + |   |   |   | 2W |   |   |
|   | 2W |   |   |   | 3L |   |   | L | 3L |   |   |   | 2W |   |
| 3W |   |   | 2L |   |   |   | B | L | I | T | Z | I | N | G |

**41.**

JOKE, AJAR, RAJA and BENJ; JEWEL, FJORD, RAJAH, BANJO and SAMAJ. SAMAJ is in *Webster's Third New International Dictionary*, and the other words are reasonably common.

**42.**

DOORMAN and MADRONO.

**43.**

MADRONA and ROADMAN.

**44.**

PROTOZOON is one of a very small number of examples.

**45.**

OWING gives LOWING, ROWING, VOWING and WOWING.

**46.**

XYST, AXLE, TAXI and FLEX; XENON, EXIST, BUXOM, ATAXY and INDEX.

**47.**

ATHIRST, RATTISH and TARTISH.

**48.**

EARPLUG.

**49.**

EDITORS, ROISTED, ROSITED, SORTIED, STEROID, STORIED and TRIODES.

**50.**

A – PANDORA; E – OPERAND; I – PONIARD; O – PANDOOR; and U – PANDOUR.

**51.**

| | | | |
|---|---|---|---|
| REGALIA | SPRUCY | LAITY | PENALTIES |
| ANALOG | INLACED | PLANE | URANISM |
| RUMBA | SERIAL | REIGN | ENEMY |
| ERECT | | | |

**52.**

Play the following six moves:

| | | |
|---|---|---|
| 1. | CIGS (C = blank) | 8 |
| 2. | CIGS | 7 |
| 3. | SEZ (Z = blank) | 2 |
| 4. | SEZ | 2 |
| 5. | ES | 2 |
| 6. | GOES, GOES | 12 |

**53.**

ZEAL, CZAR, DAZE and WHIZ; ZEBRA, AZOIC, UNZIP, FROZE and WALTZ.

**54.**

In the game shown here, 1,112 points have been scored. The words played are as follows:

|    |                      |     |
|----|----------------------|-----|
| 1. | STROLLS              | 66  |
| 2. | DO                   | 3   |
| 3. | DON                  | 4   |
| 4. | ORT, ST              | 7   |
| 5. | PRONGHORN            | 221 |
| 6. | OD                   | 3   |
| 7. | ODD                  | 10  |
| 8. | LONGS (O = blank)    | 7   |
| 9. | OFF, FLONGS          | 27  |
| 10.| TOFF                 | 10  |
| 11.| OB                   | 4   |
| 12.| LOB                  | 5   |
| 13.| BLOB                 | 8   |
| 14.| COXCOMBS             | 284 |
| 15.| OR                   | 4   |
| 16.| ORT                  | 3   |

| C | O | X | C | O | M | B | S |   |   |   | 2 L |   |   | W |
|---|---|---|---|---|---|---|---|---|---|---|-----|---|---|---|
|   | R |   |   | N | 3 L | L |   |   | 3 L |   |   | D | Z | O |
|   | T | 2 W |   |   | T | O | F | F |   |   |   | 2 W |   | R |
| 2 L |   |   | 2 W |   |   | B | 2 L | L |   |   | J |   |   | K |
|   |   |   |   | 2 W |   |   | T | + | W | M | + | N | T | S |
|   | 3 L |   |   |   | 3 L |   |   | N | 3 L |   | G |   | 3 L | H |
| P |   | 2 L |   |   | D | 2 L |   | G |   |   |   | 2 L |   | O |
| R |   | S | T | R | O | L | L | S |   |   | 2 L |   |   | P |
| O | R | T |   |   | N | 2 L |   | 2 L |   |   |   | 2 L |   |   |
| N | 3 L |   |   | 3 L |   |   |   | 3 L |   |   |   | 3 L |   |   |
| G |   |   | 2 W |   |   |   |   |   | 2 W |   |   |   |   |   |
| H |   | 2 W |   |   |   | 2 L |   |   |   | 2 W |   |   | 2 L |   |
| O | D | D |   |   | 2 L |   | 2 L |   |   | 2 W |   |   |   |   |
| R | 2 W |   |   | 3 L |   |   | 3 L |   |   |   |   | 2 W |   |   |
| N |   | 2 L |   |   | 3 W |   |   |   | 2 L |   |   |   | 3 W |   |

| | |
|---|---:|
| 17. ON | 2 |
| 18. TOWMONTS (both Os = blanks) | 72 |
| 19. JO | 16 |
| 20. JOG | 10 |
| 21. WORKSHOP | 311 |
| 22. ZO | 22 |
| 23. DZO | 13 |
| Total | 1,112 |

**55.**

1,604 points is possible. Play the ten bird names as shown below and in the diagram here:

1. LORIOTS 64
2. SERIEMAS 56
3. BUNTINGS 72
4. LOVEBIRD 78
5. AMADAVAT 78
6. ORTOLANS 66
7. PAROQUET 311
8. HOATZINS 320
9. JACKDAWS 320
10. WHIMBREL 239

| W | H | I | M | B | R | E | L | | | 2L | | | | J |
|---|---|---|---|---|---|---|---|---|---|---|---|---|---|---|
| | 2W | | | U | 3L | | | 3L | | | | 2W | | A |
| | | 2W | | N | 2L | | 2L | | | | | 2W | | C |
| 2L | | | 2W | T | | | 2L | | | | | 2W | | K |
| | | | | I | | | L | O | V | E | B | I | R | D |
| | 3L | | | N | 3L | | O | | 3L | | | 3L | | A |
| | | 2L | | G | | 2L | R | 2L | | | 2L | | | W |
| P | | 2L | | S | E | R | I | E | M | A | S | | | S |
| A | | 2L | | | 2L | | O | 2L | | M | | 2L | | |
| R | 3L | | | 3L | | | T | 3L | | A | | 3L | | |
| O | R | T | O | L | A | N | S | | | D | | | | |
| Q | | 2W | | | 2L | | | | | A | 2W | | 2L | |
| U | | 2W | | | 2L | | 2L | | | V | | 2W | | |
| E | 2W | | | 3L | | | 3L | | | A | | 2W | | |
| T | | | 2L | | | | H | O | A | T | Z | I | N | S |

**56.**
ACIDIFIABLE is one of very few examples.


**57.**
EMIGRES, REGIMES and REMIGES.


**58.**
The best here is a mere five, using DEEINX.

| | | | |
|---|---|---|---|
| D | INDEXED | S | INDEXES |
| F | ENFIXED | V | INVEXED |
| R | INDEXER | | |


**59.**
ALLERGY, GALLERY, LARGELY and REGALLY.


**60.**
There is not a valid Scrabble word that can be made from the letters of IRELAND. There are a number of proper names, but these are not allowed, of course.


**61.**
BEACHED, DEBACLE, DEBAUCH, CARBIDE, BROCADE and CUDBEAR.


**62.**
OPERANT, PRONATE and PROTEAN.


**63.**
MUUMUU.


**64.**

| | | | | | | | |
|---|---|---|---|---|---|---|---|
| A | TEASERS | H | HEATERS | O | ROSEATE | U | NEUTERS |
| B | BEATERS | I | RECITES | P | REPEATS | V | RESTIVE |
| C | CREATES | J | JESTERS | Q | REQUEST | W | WESTERN |
| D | STEERED | K | RETAKES | R | RESTERS | X | DEXTERS |
| E | EERIEST | L | STERILE | S | TRESSES | Y | STYRENE |
| F | FEASTER | M | STEAMER | T | SETTERS | Z | SELTZER |
| G | RESTAGE | N | ENTRIES | | | | |

**65.**

In the game shown here, 702 points have been scored. The words played are as follows:

| | | |
|---|---|---:|
| 1. | SH | 10 |
| 2. | UNCLUTCH (second U = blank) | 70 |
| 3. | UN | 2 |
| 4. | TRUNKFULS | 230 |
| 5. | UG | 3 |
| 6. | CRWTH, UGH | 40 |
| 7. | TRUSTFUL (both Us = blanks) | 68 |
| 8. | UNTRUSTFUL | 11 |
| 9. | MUGWUMPS | 248 |
| 10. | DUX | 10 |
| 11. | UP | 8 |
| 12. | ST | 2 |
| | Total | 702 |

| | | | | | | | | | | | | | | |
|---|---|---|---|---|---|---|---|---|---|---|---|---|---|---|
| **M** | | | 2L | | | **T** | **R** | **U** | **N** | **K** | **F** | **U** | **L** | **S** |
| **U** | **P** | | | | 3L | | | **N** | 3L | | | | **G** | 2W |
| **G** | | 2W | | | | 2L | | **C** | **R** | **W** | **T** | **H** | | |
| **W** | | | 2W | **D** | | | 2L | **L** | | | 2W | | | 2L |
| **U** | **N** | **T** | **R** | **+** | **S** | **T** | **F** | **+** | **L** | 2W | | | | |
| **M** | 3L | | | **X** | 3L | | | **T** | 3L | | | | 3L | |
| **P** | | 2L | | | | 2L | | **C** | | | | 2L | | |
| **S** | **T** | | 2L | | | | **S** | **H** | | | 2L | | | 3W |
| | | 2L | | | | 2L | | 2L | | | | 2L | | |
| | 3L | | | 3L | | | | 3L | | | | | 3L | |
| | | | 2W | | | | | | 2W | | | | | |
| 2L | | | 2W | | | | 2L | | | | 2W | | | 2L |
| | | 2W | | | | 2L | | 2L | | | | 2W | | |
| | 2W | | | | 3L | | | | 3L | | | | 2W | |
| 3W | | | 2L | | | | 3W | | | | 2L | | | 3W |

213

**66.**
ZOOSPOROUS is one of a tiny number of possibilities.

**67.**

| | | | |
|---|---|---|---|
| ATINGLE | FELTING | MELTING | SINGLET |
| ELATING | ENLIGHT | LENTIGO | TINGLES |
| GELATIN | LIGHTEN | PELTING | ETTLING |
| GENITAL | LIGNITE | RINGLET | LETTING |
| BELTING | JINGLET | TINGLER | ELUTING |
| GLINTED | KINGLET | TRINGLE | WELTING |
| TINGLED | TELLING | GLISTEN | WINGLET |
| GENTILE | | | |

**68.**
SMARAGD.

**69.**
ELOHIST, EOLITHS, HOLIEST and HOSTILE.

**70.**
EIOSTZ combines with seven letters.

| | | | |
|---|---|---|---|
| A | AZOTISE | I | ZOISITE |
| C | COZIEST | O | OOZIEST |
| D | DOZIEST | U | OUTSIZE |
| F | FOZIEST | | |

# SOLUTIONS TO FOREIGN SCRABBLE PUZZLES

## DUTCH SCRABBLE PUZZLES

1. Play ERNSTIG, AARDE and ZIJN for 121 points.
2. Using the E of ARE, play JALOEZIE for 108 points.

## GERMAN SCRABBLE PUZZLES

1. Using the R of ODER, play ERSUCHEN and ER for 88 points.
2. Using the T of GEÜBT, and using the blank as an A, play TRAUMHAFT for 86 points.

## GREEK SCRABBLE PUZZLES

1. Play ΓΡΑΦΙΤΗΣ for 120 points.
2. Using the E of ΕΤΑΙΡΟΣ, play ΧΕΖΩ for 90 points.

## RUSSIAN SCRABBLE PUZZLES

1. Play КАЧЕСТВО for 96 points.
2. Using А of ЛМАР, play ЩАДНТЬ for 78 points.

## SPANISH SCRABBLE PUZZLES

1. Play CHISTERA, ASPAR and IRA for 108 points.
2. Play CUAJO and CERA for 52 points.

# BIBLIOGRAPHY

There are very few books specifically geared to the game of Scrabble itself. The few that do exist are mentioned in the first part of the bibliography.

The second part of the bibliography deals with books which contain some reference to Scrabble, but which are not devoted to the game.

The third part of the bibliography is devoted to English dictionaries and word-lists. With just one exception, *The Official Scrabble Players Dictionary*, none of these is particularly aimed at Scrabble players. This section contains a number of major English-language dictionaries, of varying sizes and of varying ages. This third part of the bibliography also includes a variety of word-lists in which words are listed in sequences other than those found in a standard dictionary. For example, *Chambers Words* lists all two-letter words together, then all three-letter words, then all four-letter words, and so on. Another example, *Longman Crossword Key*, gives all words of the same length together, but lists them according to their second letters, then their third letters, and so on. One last example, *The Word Game Winning Dictionary* lists all words against their 'alphabetically reduced' forms; in other words, the word TRAINEE would appear as an entry against the letter sequence AEEINRT. Most of these word-lists are aimed at crossword puzzle enthusiasts and other word-puzzlers. None of them, with the exception of *The Official Scrabble Players Dictionary*, mentions Scrabble players as a part of their target audience.

The fourth part of the bibliography lists a small number of foreign-language dictionaries. These are particularly useful for solving the foreign-language Scrabble puzzles in this book.

# SPECIFICALLY SCRABBLE

Brandreth, Gyles. *The Complete Book of Scrabble*, published by Robert Hale, London, 1980 (hardback) and Sphere, London, 1981 (paperback) (the paperback edition contains various amendments and corrections to the material in the hardback edition)

Brandreth, Gyles. *The Scrabble Puzzle Book*, published by Queen Anne Press, London, 1981

Conklin, Drue. *The Scrabble Players Handbook*, published by Harmony Books, New York, 1975

Francis, Darryl. *Scrabble, Know The Game*, published by EP Publishing, West Yorkshire, 1974.

Francis, Darryl. *Word Rules*, published by the London Scrabble League, London, 1982

Goldman, Michael. *Play Better Scrabble*, published by the author, London, 1983.

Hinch, Derryn. *The Scrabble Book*, published by Mason/ Charter, New York, 1976

Orleans, Jacob and Jacobson, Edmund. *How to Win at Scrabble*, published by Hodder and Stoughton, London, 1955

Orleans, Jacob and Jacobson, Edmund. *The Scrabble Word Guide*, published by Hodder and Stoughton, London, 1955

Orleans, Jacob and Jacobson, Edmund. *More Fun with Scrabble*, published by Hodder and Stoughton, London, 1955

Richter, Alan. *Championship Scrabble*, published by Kaye and Ward, London, 1980

Turcan, Peter. *A Competitive Scrabble Program*, available from Department of Computer Science, University of Reading, Reading, England (this was written in 1981, and is a paper produced as part of a PhD thesis, 1979–82)

## LIMITED REFERENCE TO SCRABBLE

Ainslie, Tom. *Ainslie's Complete Hoyle*, published by New English Library, London, 1977

Borgmann, Dmitri. *Beyond Language*, published by Charles Scribner's Sons, New York, 1967

Brandreth, Gyles. *The Joy of Lex*, published by William Morrow, New York, 1980

Brandreth, Gyles. *More Joy of Lex*, published by William Morrow, New York, 1982

The Diagram Group. *The Way to Play*, published by Bantam, London, 1977

Eckler, Ross. *Word Recreations*, published by Dover, New York, 1979

Millington, Roger. *The Strange World of the Crossword*, published by M and J Hobbs, London, 1974

Morehead, Albert and Mott-Smith, Geoffrey (editors). *Hoyle's Rules of Games*, published by Signet, New York, 1965

Parlett, David. *The Penguin Book of Word Games*, published by
    Penguin, Middlesex, England, 1982
Silverman, David. *Your Move*, published by Kaye and Ward,
    London, 1973


# ENGLISH LANGUAGE DICTIONARIES AND WORD-LISTS


*The American Heritage Dictionary of the English Language*,
    Second College Edition, published by Houghton Mifflin,
    New York, 1982
*The Anagram Dictionary*, by Michael Curl, published by Robert
    Hale, London, 1982
*Cassell's Crossword Finisher*, by John Griffiths, published by
    Cassell, London, 1975
*Chambers Twentieth Century Dictionary*, edited by Betty
    Kirkpatrick, published by Chambers, Edinburgh, 1972 and
    1983
*Chambers Words*, introduced by Frank Muir, published by
    Chambers, Edinburgh, 1976
*Collins English Dictionary*, published by Collins, London, 1983
*The Concise Oxford Dictionary*, edited by J. B. Sykes, published
    by Oxford University Press, Oxford, Seventh Edition, 1982
*Crossword Anagram Dictionary*, by R. J. Edwards, published by
    Barrie and Jenkins, London, 1978
*Dictionary of Anagrams*, by Samuel Hunter, published by
    Routledge and Kegan Paul, London, 1982
*Funk and Wagnall's Crossword Puzzle Finder*, by Edmund
    Schwartz and Leon Landovitz, published by Stonesong
    Press, New York, 1979
*Funk and Wagnall's New Standard Dictionary of the English
    Language*, published by Funk and Wagnall, New York,
    1946
*Funk and Wagnall's Standard College Dictionary*, published by
    Funk and Wagnall, New York, 1973
*Hamlyn Encyclopedic World Dictionary*, published by Hamlyn,
    London, 1971
*Longman Crossword Key*, by Evelyn Marshall, published by
    Longman, Essex, England, 1982
*The Oxford English Dictionary*, published by Oxford University
    Press, Oxford, 1933
*A Supplement to the Oxford English Dictionary*, edited by
    Robert Burchfield, published by Oxford University Press,

Oxford (volume 1, A–G, 1972; volume 2, H–N, 1976; and volume 3, O–Scz, 1982)

*The Official Scrabble Players Dictionary*, published by G. & C. Merriam, Springfield, Massachusetts, 1978

*The Random House Dictionary of the English Language*, Unabridged Edition, edited by Jess Stein, published by Random House, New York, 1966

*The Shorter Oxford English Dictionary*, edited by C. T. Onions, published by Oxford University Press, Oxford, Third Edition, 1973

*Webster's New Collegiate Dictionary*, published by G. & C. Merriam, Springfield, Massachusetts, Seventh Edition, 1970; Eighth Edition, 1973; Ninth Edition, 1983

*Webster's New International Dictionary of the English Language*, Second Edition, edited by William Neilson, published by G. & C. Merriam, Springfield, Massachusetts, 1934

*Webster's Third New International Dictionary of the English Language*, edited by Philip Gove, published by G. & C. Merriam, Springfield, Massachusetts, 1961

*The Word Game Winning Dictionary*, by Bruce Wetterau, published by Signet, New York, 1980

# FOREIGN LANGUAGE DICTIONARIES

*Collins Gem Russian–English English–Russian Dictionary*, by Waldemer Schapiro, published by Collins, London, 1963

*Concise Dutch and English Dictionary*, by Peter and Margaretha King, published by Hodder and Stoughton, London, 1958

*The Concise French Dictionary*, edited by Francesca Langbaum, published by Random House, New York, 1954

*The Concise German Dictionary*, edited by Jenni Karding Moulton, published by Random House, New York, 1959

*The Concise Italian Dictionary*, edited by Robert Hall Jr, published by Random House, New York, 1957

*The Concise Spanish Dictionary*, edited by Donald Sola, published by Random House, New York, 1954

*A Greek–English Dictionary*, published by Alex and E. Papademetriou, Athens, undated